The Politics and Economics of Public Spending

THE H. ROWAN GAITHER LECTURES
IN SYSTEMS SCIENCE

are named in memory of one of the founders
and the first Chairman of the Board of the RAND Corporation.
They were established by gift of the System Development Corporation,
formerly a division of the RAND Corporation,
and are arranged by the Graduate School of Business Administration
and the Center for Research in Management Science
of the University of California, Berkeley.
Charles J. Hitch was the first lecturer in the series.
Charles L. Schultze was the second.

CHARLES L. SCHULTZE

The Politics and Economics of Public Spending

H. Rowan Gaither Lectures, delivered May 1968,
at the University of California, Berkeley,
under the sponsorship of the Graduate School
of Business Administration and the Center
for Research in Management Science

THE BROOKINGS INSTITUTION *Washington, D.C.*

THE BROOKINGS INSTITUTION
is an independent organization devoted to non-partisan research, education, and publication in economics, government, foreign policy, and the social sciences generally. Its principal purposes are to aid in the development of sound public policies and to promote public understanding of issues of national importance.

The Institution was founded on December 8, 1927, to merge the activities of the Institute for Government Research, founded in 1916, the Institute of Economics, founded in 1922, and the Robert Brookings Graduate School of Economics and Government, founded in 1924.

The general administration of the Institution is the responsibility of a self-perpetuating Board of Trustees. The trustees are likewise charged with maintaining the independence of the staff and fostering the most favorable conditions for creative research and education. The immediate direction of the policies, program, and staff of the Institution is vested in the President, assisted by an advisory council chosen from the staff of the Institution.

In publishing a study, the Institution presents it as a competent treatment of a subject worthy of public consideration. The interpretations and conclusions in such publications are those of the author or authors and do not purport to represent the views of the other staff members, officers, or trustees of the Brookings Institution.

Foreword

One-fifth of the national income of the United States flows through the federal budget. Our security; our progress in reducing poverty, hunger, and disease; the purity of the air we breathe and the water we drink; the safety of the roads we drive on and the airlanes we fly—all these and countless other aspects of our national well-being are affected by the decisions made in the budget.

In recent years a major effort has been made to bring modern techniques of management and analysis to bear on federal budget decisions. While improvements in budget practice have been gradually occurring over the years, they received a major new impetus in 1961 when the incoming Secretary of Defense, Robert S. McNamara, established the planning, programming, and budgeting system (PPB) in the Department of Defense. The system was devised as a means of providing policy makers with an analytic evaluation of existing and proposed programs, buttressed wherever possible with quantitative measures of performance. In 1965, President Johnson directed that PPB be adopted by the civilian agencies of the federal government in the preparation of their budget requests.

Most of the important budgetary decisions the federal government is called upon to make, however, are not just technical decisions. How budgetary issues are decided affects the cherished values and vital interests of individuals and groups. In a democracy, the political tools of decision making—bargaining, advocacy, negotiation, and compromise—are the means by which workable arrangements are made amid conflict about values and interests.

In this book the author examines the relation between the analytical and political approaches to budgetary decisions. He seeks to define the role of PPB, of the professional expert, and of modern management techniques in the essentially political process by which government decisions are made. By spelling out the contributions and limitations of the two approaches, he suggests how each can complement the other.

Charles L. Schultze, a Brookings senior fellow and Director of the Bureau of the Budget under President Johnson, presented the material in this book as the second series of H. Rowan Gaither Memorial Lectures in Systems Science at the University of California at Berkeley in the spring of 1968.

The author owes a debt of gratitude to those of his colleagues who commented on earlier versions of the lectures. Particular thanks are due to William M. Capron, Herbert Kaufman, Martin C. McGuire, Joseph A. Pechman, Allen Schick, and Gilbert Y. Steiner. He is also grateful to Susan Gilbert for thorough and sympathetic editorial review, to Evelyn P. Fisher whose painstaking care prevented many factual errors, to John Dowling for research assistance, and to Florence Robinson for preparing the index.

The views expressed in this book are those of the author. They do not necessarily reflect the views of the trustees, the officers, or other staff members of the Brookings Institution.

KERMIT GORDON
President

December 1968
Washington, D.C.

Contents

The Politics and Economics of Public Spending

1 The Evolution of Budgetary Techniques

Charles J. Hitch inaugurated the H. Rowan Gaither Lecture Series in the spring of 1965 with a brilliant exposition of the contribution of systematic analysis in improving the process of decision making in the Department of Defense. When he spoke, the Pentagon's planning, programming, and budgeting system was approaching its fourth anniversary. Its installation in 1961 had been preceded by over a decade of work by the RAND Corporation and others on the application of systematic analysis to defense problems. Mr. Hitch not only outlined the characteristics of a "desirable" defense planning and programming system and its associated cost-effectiveness studies, but also cited the contributions which the system and the studies had already made to the decision process and to specific defense decisions.

In August 1965, almost coincident with the first Gaither Lectures, President Lyndon B. Johnson directed all the major civilian agencies of the federal government to install planning, programming, and budgeting systems (PPB) along the general lines of the Defense Department model. He also instructed each agency to establish a central program policy and planning staff to assist in designing the system and carrying out its planning and analytic functions.[1]

In this second series of Gaither Lectures I will examine how long-term planning and systematic analysis have been applied to the federal government's civilian programs. These lectures complement those of Mr. Hitch, but they will differ in basic content since I will deal principally with the question of whether and how PPB as a system, and cost effectiveness as an analytic technique, can fit into the political decision-making process.

You may be surprised that I use the phrase "whether . . . PPB

1. Statement by the President to members of the cabinet and heads of agencies, August 25, 1965.

1

. . . can fit into the political decision-making process." To the economist imbued with the problem of efficiency, or to the systems analyst accustomed to a problem-solving approach, this question may appear trivial. Clearly the nation is faced with a variety of domestic problems and domestic needs that can be met only through governmental action. The federal government has mounted a number of programs addressed to those wants and problems. Limited funds must be allocated among programs. Many program objectives can be reached only by the application of resources over a number of years. To reach any given objective, some means are more effective than others. What could be more clearly needed in budgetary allocation and program design than long-term planning and careful, systematic analysis of alternative means of achieving objectives?

Let me assure you, the question I have posed is not trivial, either to political scientists or, what is more important, to practicing political decision makers. The process by which decisions are reached in the federal government has been developed over a period of almost two centuries. It is an amazingly sophisticated means of reaching a workable consensus among groups who hold quite diverse, vaguely specified, but intensely felt political values—about education, farm prices, postal subsidies, income distribution, law enforcement, urban transportation, and every other subject that is a candidate for government action, or inaction.

PPB and cost-effectiveness analysis are designed to solve problems by finding the most effective and most efficient solution on the basis of objective criteria. The essence of political decision making, on the other hand, is to reach agreement among individuals and groups whose values and objectives may differ substantially. Political values permeate every aspect of the decision-making process in the majority of federal domestic programs. There is no simple division of labor in which the "politicians" achieve consensus on an agreed-on set of objectives while the "analysts" design and evaluate—from efficiency and effectiveness criteria—alternative means of achieving those objectives.

As experience in the Defense Department has taught us, systematic analysis is itself intimately concerned with the specification of objectives. In his lectures on analysis for military decisions, E. S. Quade stressed that systems analysis "is associated with that class of problems where the difficulty lies in deciding what ought to be done—not simply how to do it—and honors go to people who . . . find out what the problem is."[2] Or as Charles Hitch put it, "We must learn to look at objectives as critically and as professionally as we look at our models and our other inputs."[3]

Moreover, the choice of means, particularly among domestic programs, is almost equally as freighted with political values as is the choice of ends. While the decision to pursue the development of an antiballistic missile system (ABM) is a highly political decision, in that it involves judgments about important national objectives, the technical design of an effective ABM system is not loaded with political values. In most domestic programs, however, decisions about "means" are often no less political than decisions about "ends." In such programs it is impossible to assume that once objectives or ends have been chosen, technical analysis can proceed unhindered to select the most effective means to achieve those ends. Whether, for example, the federal government helps to increase the future supply of health personnel by providing financial assistance to medical students, by

2. E. S. Quade (ed.), *Analysis for Military Decisions* (Rand McNally, 1964), p. 7.
3. Charles J. Hitch, "On the Choice of Objectives in Systems Studies," P–1955 (processed; Santa Monica, Calif.: RAND Corporation, 1960), p. 19.

making construction grants-in-aid to medical schools, by the support of research at medical schools, or by the encouragement of paramedical skills is a decision carrying with it a number of political consequences.

As a more dramatic illustration, the congressional authorization for the Department of Defense's procurement and research and development programs—$22 billion in fiscal 1969—is contained on one page. While I have not made a specific check, it would be conservative to estimate that the statutes authorizing an equivalent $22 billion of programs in the Department of Health, Education, and Welfare (HEW) take up several shelves of a bookcase. There are some fifty different appropriations covering the $78 billion expenditures in the military functions of the Department of Defense. For the $14.5 billion spent by HEW (outside of the trust funds) there are approximately one hundred different appropriations—less than one-fifth the funds but twice the number of appropriations.

The detailed control of civilian budget expenditures by Congress simply reflects the fact that even minor decisions about the means of achieving social ends intimately affect income distribution, political power relationships, and group attitudes toward social questions.[4]

In my own view, PPB and systematic analysis can improve— and indeed already have improved—the quality of program design and the allocation of budgetary resources within the civilian

4. The example of the ABM can be extended to clarify the distinction I am making. I have argued that although the decision to deploy an ABM is as political as any other major national decision, the technical choice of hardware to carry out that decision is much less political than the choice of technical program details in civilian programs. But should a decision be made to extend the ABM beyond its present "area defense" role against a Red Chinese threat and to employ it to protect individual American cities against a Soviet attack, then the choice of which cities to protect with "point defense" will be as intensely political as any decision can be.

sector of the government. But the role of PPB in the political process needs to be carefully defined. It needs to be defended against those political pragmatists who dismiss it as an academic exercise incompatible with political reality and therefore doomed to failure. It also needs to be defended against ardent enthusiasts who, failing to understand the environment in which PPB must operate and finding that planning and analysis seldom bear a one-to-one relationship with subsequent decisions, become disillusioned, give up the fight, and turn to other pursuits muttering about the perfidy of politicians.

These lectures, therefore, will deal mainly, though not exclusively, with an examination of how planning and analysis fit into the political decision-making process which characterizes federal civilian programs. The first step is to examine briefly how PPB relates to and builds upon earlier improvements in budgetary techniques.

PPB can best be viewed as part of an evolutionary process within which federal budgetary techniques have developed. While it is a major step, and in some respects makes a quantum jump from the past, it is still part of a development that has been going on by fits and starts for fifty years.

There are three major roles that can be distinguished for a budget:[5]

Financial control: the control of subordinate units to insure that public funds are spent only for those objects or purposes specified by law and that appropriations are not exceeded.

5. This threefold classification is taken from Robert N. Anthony, *Planning and Control Systems; A Framework for Analysis* (Harvard University Press, 1965), pp. 16–18. What I have labeled "financial control," Anthony called "operational control." The relationship traced in the following pages between PPB and this threefold classification owes a great deal to Allen Schick's perceptive article, "The Road to PPB: The Stages of Budget Reform," *Public Administration Review*, Vol. XXVI, No. 4 (December 1966), pp. 243–58.

Observance of statutory restrictions, adherence to the fund provided in appropriations acts, and avoidance of corruption are the basic objectives of financial control.

Managerial control: programming the use of resources—manpower, equipment, transportation, and the like—to carry out an approved set of activities in an efficient manner. Procurement regulations that minimize purchase costs, work measurement programs designed to raise output per man-hour, streamlining of paper processing, and introduction of labor-saving equipment are among the typical activities encompassed by the management control function.

Strategic planning: establishing and specifying objectives, choosing among alternative programs to achieve those objectives, and allocating resources among those programs. Strategic planning is concerned with the determination of the kind and level of activities that managerial control seeks to carry out efficiently.

Both financial and managerial controls take the objectives of federal programs, their design and specification, and the level at which they are carried out as given. The purpose of these controls is to insure that approved programs are operated honestly, efficiently, and according to the provisions of the law. Strategic planning, however, brings into the budgetary process precisely those decisions about program objectives, specifications, and level which are taken as given in the financial and managerial control functions.

Until the 1920s, no overall executive budget existed and none of the three major functions of budgeting was effectively performed. The President had no institutional system or central staff resources to exert operational or managerial control over the various federal agencies. Each agency presented its budget requests directly to the Congress. The President had no systematic means of controlling the size or composition of those requests. He could intervene through his cabinet on an ad hoc basis, but this was not common practice. Decisions on the allocation of funds flowed directly from the appropriation actions of the Congress, which did not have before it the President's recommendations.

Executive operations did not begin this way. In the early days of the Republic, Alexander Hamilton managed to establish a central executive budget. All funds made available by the Congress for the entire federal government were contained in four broad appropriations: one to cover the civil list, one for the Army and Navy, one to pay outstanding Treasury warrants, and one to encompass all other federal activities. Such an arrangement suited Hamilton's desire for a strong central government, and within that government a strong executive to face the Congress. These early budgetary arrangements gave broad discretion to the executive, and contained the potential for development of a centrally planned budget and a deliberate allocation of resources among competing agencies.

The Congress soon became disenchanted with this arrangement. Jefferson, supporting the Congress, said in his first congressional message:

In our care, too, of the public contributions entrusted to our direction it would be prudent to multiply barriers against their dissipation by appropriating specific sums to every specific purpose susceptible of definition; by disallowing all applications of money varying from the appropriation or transcending it in amount; by reducing the undefined field of contingencies and thereby circumscribing discretionary powers over money . . .[6]

Jefferson's views prevailed. The concept of an executive budget, with relatively broad appropriation categories, was soon

6. Cited in Arthur Smithies, *The Budgetary Process in the United States* (McGraw-Hill, 1955), p. 51.

replaced by detailed congressional supervision over the objects of expenditure. With only minor exceptions—particularly during wars—the budgetary system of the United States from 1800 to 1921 could be described as having the following characteristics:

1. Budget requests were submitted to the Congress directly by the individual federal agencies. The President had no authority to amend those requests before they were submitted and no institutional mechanism to influence the departments in drawing up the requests.

2. Appropriations were made in great detail. During most of the period the executive had little authority to make transfers among appropriation accounts.

3. The great detail in which appropriations were made, the inability of department heads to transfer funds, and the lack of any central control mechanism led to the widespread growth of deficiency appropriations. Department heads and subordinate bureau chiefs often made contracts and commitments in excess of appropriated funds and subsequently presented the bills to Congress.

4. The Congress was principally concerned with limiting the power and discretion of the executive by specifying appropriations in detail and by controlling the tendency of executive departments to sidestep these restrictions through deficiency appropriations. "Keep your hands out of the cookie jar" and "Keep spending within appropriation limits" were the two commandments. Efficient execution of programs and effective pursuit of objectives were not the primary concern.

The first major change in the system came with the Budget and Accounting Act of 1921. The act established an executive budget for the first time since Hamilton. The President rather than the individual department was to submit budget requests to the Congress. The budget became the President's budget. The

Bureau of the Budget was established in the Treasury Department—but with independent access to the President and substantial power with respect to individual departments. The General Accounting Office was established as a congressional arm to determine accounting procedures for federal finances and to act as an audit agency.

This act was preceded by two amazingly advanced studies of the budgetary process. The New York Bureau of Municipal Research in 1907 recommended a threefold set of budgetary classifications.[7] Classification *by function*—such as health, education, law enforcement—would assist in setting the nature and level of programs and would provide data for the evaluation of results. Functional classification emphasizes "what" is to be done. Classification *by work programs*—furnishing data by organizational unit and type of activity in order to assist managerial control—would give detailed schedules of activities upon which work measurement programs and productivity improvements could be based. Work programs classification emphasizes "how" activities are to be carried out. Classification *by objects of expenditure*—personnel, equipment, and travel—would provide financial controls over subordinate officials charged with spending funds and would help keep expenditures within the limits of appropriations. Classification by objects emphasizes the audit and control aspects of budgeting.

This was indeed an advanced concept of budgeting. It recognized the three different functions of budgeting—control, management, and planning. And the bureau's proposal was designed to provide the necessary information in the relevant categories to carry out these divided functions.

In 1911, President Taft appointed a Commission on Economy

7. Cited in Schick, "The Road to PPB," p. 244.

and Efficiency. The commission's report in 1912 (H. Doc. 458, 62 Cong. 2 sess.) was a far-sighted document. It opposed appropriations by object class, rightly arguing that line itemization of expenditure objects, particularly when done in great detail, eliminated the flexibility needed by the executive to improve the efficiency with which governmental activities were carried out. Instead the commission recommended a multidimensional set of budgetary accounts, along lines proposed by the New York Bureau of Municipal Research.

In one of his last acts as President, Taft submitted to the Congress a model budget based on the recommendations of the commission. Expenditures were classified by function, by organizational unit, by type of activity, and were subdivided between capital and current account. Moreover, extensive cross-classification among these categories was provided. It was indeed a model budget.

In 1918, W. F. Willoughby of the Brookings Institution published a proposal for an executive budget constructed along similar lines. Willoughby also recommended the creation of an executive branch agency to prepare, oversee, and audit the budget.[8]

Nothing was done about budgetary reform, however, until the Budget and Accounting Act of 1921. While a central executive budget and a Bureau of the Budget in the Treasury Department were established, the far-ranging recommendations of the Taft Commission were not put into effect. Under its first two directors, General Charles G. Dawes (1921–22) and General H. M. Lord (1922–29), the new bureau concentrated most of its efforts toward carrying out the financial control function. Budgeting was completely divorced from policy making and program deci-

8. William F. Willoughby, *The Problem of a National Budget* (New York: Institute for Government Research, 1918).

sions. The broader aspects of management were ignored in favor of paper clip efficiency.

A sense of the spirit and early practice of executive budgeting can be gleaned from the speeches of Generals Dawes and Lord during the 1920s.[9]

We in the Bureau of the Budget are not concerned with matters of policy. The President, advised by the Cabinet, and Congress determine the great questions of policy. As for us, we are men down in the stokehole of the ship of state, and we are concerned simply with the economical handling of fuel. (Dawes)

I want to say here again that the Budget Bureau keeps humble, and if it ever becomes obsessed with the idea that it has any work except to save money and improve efficiency in routine business it will cease to be useful in the hands of the President. Again I say, we have nothing to do with policy. (Dawes)

Investigation by a representative of the department of which the bureau was a part disclosed loss or theft of towels by the hundred, while more than 500 soiled towels were discovered tucked away in desks, file cases, and closets. The simple and obvious requirement that an employee turn in a soiled towel in order to secure a clean one was immediately put into effect. In this same bureau there was great consumption of soap. Five barrels of Government soap were located in the home of one of the bureau employees and three barrels in the home of another. These industrious soap collectors are no longer in the Federal service. . . . In this bureau was discovered the enterprising employee with the elastic conscience who made from Government rubber bands a 10-pound ball as a plaything for his dog. He has now ample time for playing with the ball himself. (Lord)

9. All of the quotes are from *Addresses of the President of the United States and the Director of the Bureau of the Budget*, Regular Meeting of the Business Organization of the Government. They are from Second Semiannual Meeting, February 3, 1922, pp. 13, 14; Fifth Regular Meeting, June 18, 1923, p. 15; Ninth Regular Meeting, June 22, 1925, pp. 15–16, respectively.

The General Supply Committee here in Washington fell heir to seven barrels of spoiled, soused seal shoulders shipped from Alaska. They were unfit for consumption. The obvious course, and the course that would have been followed a few years ago, would be to throw them away. We have to-day, however, in the Federal service frugal-minded people who have a heart for the taxpayer. One of these conservators found a market for the shoulders. They were sold for crab bait, yielding the Government $20. (Lord)

It is not really surprising that so much attention was given to the control function and the narrower aspects of the management function. When government activities are limited and considered primarily as a necessary evil, the question of the social value of benefits from government programs is not likely to arise. In the latter half of the nineteenth century federal civilian expenditures, excluding interest on the public debt and the traditional Post Office and veterans' programs, were only 2/3 of 1 percent of the gross national product (GNP). By the 1920s there had been some expansion, but these expenditures still amounted to less than 1 percent of GNP. Under these circumstances strategic planning—specification of objectives and comparison of alternative means for achieving objectives—is not likely to be given major attention. Add to this the desire of Congress to control the discretion of the executive through detailed appropriation of funds by line-item of expenditure, and there will hardly be a demand for broader concepts in formulating and carrying out an executive budget.

The sharply expanded activities of the federal government and the mushrooming of new agencies during the New Deal led to the next step in budget reform. The report of the President's Committee on Administrative Management (the Brownlow Committee, appointed in 1937) urged a substantial broadening of the budgetary role, and conceived of the budget as a means, and the Bureau of the Budget as an agent, for helping the

President manage and coordinate the increasingly complex affairs of the federal government. Largely as a result of the Brownlow Commission's recommendations, the Bureau of the Budget in 1939 was moved from the Treasury Department to an independent position in the newly created Executive Office of the President. During the subsequent fifteen years, a significant part of the bureau's energies was devoted to administrative management, particularly during the war when its role was expanded to include the administration of the war effort.

In 1949, the first Hoover Commission recommended that managerial efficiency be improved by replacing budgeting by objects of expenditure with "performance budgeting." Appropriations and expenditures should be classified according to the type of activity carried out rather than by objects of expenditure. The President should recommend and the Congress should appropriate budgetary funds among various kinds of activity— the granting of patents, the collection of taxes, the construction of water resource projects, and so forth. But within each line of activity, program managers should be free to shift resources to insure maximum efficiency. An appropriation structure that specifies how much could be spent on rent, travel, and personnel is not conducive to effective operations.

As a result of the Hoover Commission report, work measurement programs were inaugurated. The Budget and Accounting Procedures Act of 1950 directed that improvements be made in accounting systems designed to secure better cost data for each activity or work unit. These reforms were primarily aimed at improving the efficiency with which programs were executed. Progress was also made during this period in reducing the detail in which appropriations were made. Just before the Second World War there were some 2,000 individual appropriations; by 1955 this number had been reduced to 375.[10]

10. With the advent of a whole new series of programs in the 1950s and 1960s,

The budgetary reforms of the 1920s were directed toward the financial control function, while the reforms of the immediate prewar and postwar years were directed toward the managerial efficiency function. In both periods, however, primary emphasis was given to the efficient use of resources to carry out approved programs. Objectives and programs were considered given—the budgetary job was to achieve those objectives efficiently. The third round of improvements, through the planning, programming, and budgeting system, sweeps the specification of objectives, the design of programs, and the evaluation of benefits relative to costs into the budgetary process.

This is obviously an oversimplification. As the functions of the federal government expanded in number and complexity, budget decisions necessarily went beyond considerations of pure efficiency. The budget process in attempting to minimize the resource cost of a given level of activity decided on the scope of activity in that program as well. In formulating the President's budget, the allocation of resources among different programs has always involved at least an implicit evaluation of program benefits in the light of presidential objectives. Over the years the federal government increasingly came to be viewed as a means for producing valuable social outputs. In the 1960s this trend was sharply accelerated as the government accepted a wide variety of new goals and objectives in the fields of health, education, manpower training, reduction of poverty, regional economic development, and control of environmental pollution. As a percentage of GNP, federal outlays for civilian programs— apart from interest on the debt, veterans' programs, and the costs of the Post Office—rose from 1 percent or less in the 1920s

---

however, the number of individual appropriations has burgeoned again. At latest count it stands at about 1,250. David Novick (ed.), *Program Budgeting: Program Analysis and the Federal Budget* (Harvard University Press, 1965), p. 58.

to about 5 percent in the immediate postwar years and to almost 10 percent in fiscal 1969. Under these circumstances, the allocation of growing but still limited resources among competing programs necessarily brought the budget process into matters of social policy, far beyond its role in the 1920s, the 1930s, or the early postwar years.

In 1961 David Bell, then director of the budget, established "the summer preview." In essence this innovation called for a submission by each major agency to the Budget Bureau of five-year-forward financial programs, together with a discussion and analysis of program issues considered by the agency head as likely to be of major significance in subsequent budget discussions. These reports—as the name suggests—were made each summer. Ideally the midyear discussions and analysis of major issues were to form a background for the later submission of detailed budget requests.

The introduction of PPB among civilian agencies in 1965, therefore, was not the first time that the budget was used for strategic planning. Rather it recognized the fact that the actual budgetary process had been forced by the course of events to become involved in this function. When 20 percent of the national income is spent through the federal budget, the budget process must be designed to do more than exert financial control and promote management efficiency. It must also become an instrument to help policy makers assign priorities and allocate national resources among competing activities. Planning, programming, and budgeting constitutes an attempt to integrate policy formulation with budgetary resource allocation, and to provide a means for regularly bringing systematic analysis to bear on both policy formulation and budget allocation.

This third round of improvements in the budgetary process is different in kind from the first two, which were directed toward the problems of financial control and management efficiency: that is, the proper and efficient use of resources in carrying out approved programs. But, as noted earlier, PPB goes beyond matters of control and efficiency in at least three ways: (1) it is concerned with the specification of objectives and the selection of programs; (2) it presupposes that decisions on these matters can be aided by systematic analysis, using criteria which are, at least in part, not political; and (3) it establishes a planning system that tends to strengthen the authority of the upper tiers of the executive hierarchy—the President and his department heads —against the lower tiers of the hierarchy—the heads of subordinate bureaus and offices. And in so doing it significantly affects the web of relationships between the executive and the Congress.

On each of these counts, PPB impinges directly upon a complicated political process which is structured to achieve decisions by mutual adjustment among partisan advocates, each possessing different, or at least differently weighted, ends and values. Moreover, the impact of PPB upon the political process is much more pervasive in the case of most civilian programs than in defense programs.

Let me be quite careful about this distinction between defense programs and civilian programs. On matters of broad policy, defense decisions are no less political than are civilian programs. Moreover, the political problems of where facilities are located and the interests of individual firms in securing contracts play a role in all programs, defense and civilian alike. But at a lower level of decision making, political values with respect to income distribution and political power structures enter much more heavily into the detailed design of most civilian programs than in defense programs.

It is this relationship between the political process and the decision-making process as envisaged by PPB that I wish to examine. I do not believe that there is an irreconcilable conflict between the two systems. But they are different kinds of systems representing different ways of arriving at decisions. The two systems are so closely interrelated that PPB and its associated analytic method can be an effective tool for aiding decisions only when its relationships with the political process have been carefully articulated and the appropriate roles of each defined.

No one conceives of PPB as a system that makes decisions. Rather, it is a means of helping responsible officials make decisions. It is not a mechanical substitute for the good judgment, political wisdom, and the leadership of those officials. The question at issue is *not* how the PPB can supplant the political process but whether and how it can fit into that process.

2 PPB in Brief

Chapters 2 and 3 lay the groundwork for a later evaluation of PPB in the political process. Chapter 2 provides a brief description of PPB as a system for aiding the decision maker while Chapter 3 describes the political framework within which the public decision maker operates. The subsequent chapter then analyzes and compares these two aspects of decision making.

The Goals of PPB

PPB can be viewed as both a set of goals and objectives and as a system for achieving those goals. It seeks to accomplish the following ends.

First, PPB calls for careful identification and examination of goals and objectives in each major area of governmental activity. It attempts to force government agencies to step back and reflect on the fundamental aims of their current programs. For example, what are the goals of federal manpower programs? To reduce structural unemployment and inflationary pressure by retraining programs that increase the number of workers with skills in short supply? To raise the income of hard-core disadvantaged by upgrading their skills and improving their work habits? To create more job opportunities for the unskilled? While they are not wholly incompatible, they are different and the design and composition of public manpower programs will depend upon the particular combination of objectives sought.

Intercity highway programs provide another example. The objective of the intercity highway program ought not to be simply building highways. Highways are useful only to transport people and goods efficiently and safely. Once this objective is recognized, it becomes possible to analyze alternative transportation investments as means to these ends. So long as the ultimate goal of the highway program is considered the laying of

x miles of concrete, comparison of the effectiveness of various investments is impossible.

At the same time, we cannot expect the perspectives of any given level in the decision hierarchy to be as broad as those of the next higher level. The federal highway administrator will not, and should not, have the same range of objectives as the secretary of transportation nor will the secretary deal with as broad a range of alternatives as the President. Each level in the decision-making process has its own role to play. In seeking to specify program objectives, PPB aims at a realistic broadening of perspective, not at making the objectives of every participant coextensive with the President's. An attempt to force too wide a span of objectives on a participant in the process may well render the whole effort fruitless. In short, PPB seeks to encourage an analysis of program objectives in order to widen but not homogenize the perspective with which agency heads view their programs, thereby broadening the range of alternatives considered for policy and program design.

The second task of PPB is to analyze the *output* of a given program in terms of its objectives. For example, the effectiveness of various manpower training programs can only be determined in relation to a particular set of objectives. "Creaming off" the manpower pool by concentrating training resources on unemployed white high school graduates may prove highly effective when measured by the proportion of trainees subsequently employed at steady jobs and higher wages. But if the objective is to improve the lot of the hard-core unemployed or underemployed in the ghetto, comparing alternative programs on the basis of such measures of effectiveness would be inappropriate and misleading. Similarly in evaluating the highway program, it is not sufficient to ask how many miles of concrete are laid, but what the program produces in terms of safer, less-congested travel—how many hours of travel time are eliminated and how many accidents are prevented.

The third objective of PPB is the measurement of total program costs, not for just one year but for at least several years ahead. Two kinds of costs are involved. The first relates to the future budgetary consequences of current decisions. The 1968 budget, for example, requested $10 million to design a 200 billion electron volt research accelerator for the Atomic Energy Commission at an estimated construction cost of $240 million. But over a longer time period—say ten years—the total system's cost of this decision may exceed $1 billion, since operating costs, once the machine is built, will run between $60 and $100 million per year. In terms of overall budget policy it is necessary to know the extent to which future budgetary commitments are being made by current decisions. Moreover, in comparing alternative programs designed to accomplish a given objective, the comparison should be made on the basis of all the relevant costs, not just the immediate costs.

In addition to budgetary costs, there are often other costs associated with a proposed program which should be taken into account in making a decision. The costs of urban freeways, for example, are not merely the construction costs of the freeway itself but include the cost of relocating displaced residents. Even where these costs are not reflected in the budget, they are still costs to society and should be identified in the statement of program costs.

PPB, then, seeks to provide the decision maker with all the relevant costs that his decision would entail. This sounds so sensible that to belabor the point seems unnecessary. Yet too often large federal investment decisions have been made in the annual budget on the basis of only the next year's cost—or made without taking into account any of the indirectly associated costs.

A fourth and closely related goal of PPB is the formulation of objectives and programs extending beyond the single year of the annual budget submission. Most federal programs cannot achieve their intended objectives in one year. Many, like the collection of taxes, are a continuing activity some of whose components, such as the computerization of returns, have discrete time-phased objectives spread over a number of years. Others seek goals that only make sense in terms of a multiyear effort, for example, the gradual expansion of medical schools in order to bring the size of the annual graduating class to a particular level. One of the major problems of budgeting has been and remains the limited period of time covered by annual budgetary decisions. PPB seeks to relate annual budget allocations to longer-term plans.

The long-term nature of most public programs calls for long-range planning. In practice, an equally important *tactical* aspect of multiyear planning has become evident. In the short run, and in particular in the annual budget process, federal agencies are captives of the past. Prior commitments, inertia, promises to an appropriations subcommittee chairman, the need to "educate" interest-group constituents about program changes, and the like, often cause rigid constraints on yearly budget decisions. In any one year, therefore, the impact that an agency head can have on his operating bureaus is limited. By concentrating solely on what can be done in each annual budget, he can achieve very little. Major changes in objectives, operating practices, and budget allocations must be accomplished in the light of longer-range goals. By requiring subordinate bureaus to prepare the annual budget within the framework of broad, long-range budget allocations, however, the agency head can exert more influence on the general course of programs in his department than he could by fighting annual budget battles under severe constraints. Long-range budget allocations will, and should, be modified from year to year. Their value is not in their immutability, but in their use as a tool of secretarial influence over his own department. However, the role and meaning of long-range planning have been among the most troublesome aspects of PPB in civilian agencies. This problem will be discussed in Chapter 5.

The fifth and crucial aim of the PPB system is the analysis of alternatives to find the most effective means of reaching basic program objectives, and to achieve these objectives for the least cost. The goal is to force federal agencies to consider particular programs not as ends in themselves—to be perpetuated without challenge or question—but as means to objectives, subject to the competition of alternative and perhaps more effective or efficient programs. Looked at another way, PPB seeks to replace, at least in part, the pernicious practice of incremental budgeting, under which the budget allocation process does not involve a review of the basic structure of programs but primarily consists in making decisions about how much each existing program is to be increased or, much less frequently, decreased. Each program cannot, of course, be reviewed from the ground up each year. But the analytic steps of PPB call for a periodic review of fundamental program objectives, accomplishments, and costs while considering the effectiveness and efficiency of alternatives.

The sixth and final goal of PPB is to establish these analytic procedures as a systematic part of budget review. PPB seeks to subject policies and programs to analysis and to integrate the decisions into the budgetary process. Two considerations encourage this integration.

First, the allocation of limited budgetary resources among competing claims can be more intelligently made if fuller information and analysis of program objectives, effectiveness, and costs are available. When relatively narrow choices are involved

23

—such as the allocation of funds among various alternative manpower training programs—analysis can contribute directly to program decisions. But even when broader questions are being considered—such as the allocation between education and housing—analyses that present the payoffs or consequences of each program can assist the decision maker in weighing the alternatives.

Second, if it is to be more than an academic exercise, program analysis must be built into the decision-making process at each level of the decision hierarchy. By its very nature, the budget, more than any other process in the federal system, forces action. The need to formulate budget requests each year compels program decisions to be made, by the President, agency heads, bureau chiefs, and their subordinates.

These then are the aims of PPB: the specification of objectives, the evaluation of program output as it relates to objectives, the measurement of total systems costs, multiyear program planning, the evaluation of alternative program designs, and the integration of policy and program decisions with the budgetary process.

PPB as a System

The formal structure of the PPB system as it has been established in civilian agencies consists of four elements.

Program Budgeting

The activities and budgetary costs of federal programs are grouped into program categories. The literature on the desirability of these output-oriented classifications as an aid to analysis is abundant.[1] The nature of the output produced by

1. See, for example, Charles J. Hitch, "On the Choice of Objectives in Systems Studies," P-1955 (processed; Santa Monica, Calif.: RAND Corporation, 1960),

federal agencies is the key discriminant in defining program categories and assigning individual federal activities to them. Programs whose outputs are closely related, and therefore either close substitutes or necessary complements to each other, are grouped together. Broad categories such as "health," are subdivided into subcategories, such as "development of health resources" and "prevention and control of health problems." Each of the subcategories is, in turn, further subdivided into program elements. The subcategory "prevention and control of health problems," for example, contains such program elements as "mental retardation," "radiological health," and "air pollution control."

There is nothing sacred about these program classifications. They can and should be changed as analytical need dictates. Several different kinds of classifications may be needed for different analytical purposes. Their main function is to emphasize that government programs have an output, and that they should be analyzed and evaluated on the basis of how effectively and efficiently that output meets program objectives.

The set of categories appropriate to strategic planning and analysis is often quite different from the categories appropriate to the control or management efficiency functions of budgeting. A good example is found in the various classifications of the Coast Guard budget.

Appropriation categories (objects of expenditure): operating expenses; acquisition, construction, and improvements; retired pay; reserve training.

Activity schedule (types of operational processes): vessel operations; aviation operations; shore stations and aids operations; repair and supply facilities; training and recruiting facilities; administration

and Arthur Smithies, "Conceptual Framework for the Program Budget," in David Novick (ed.), *Program Budgeting: Program Analysis and the Federal Budget* (Harvard University Press, 1965), pp. 24–60.

and operational control; other military personnel expense; supporting programs.

Program budget (program outputs and objectives): search and rescue; aids to navigation; law enforcement; military readiness; merchant marine safety; oceanography and other operations; supporting services.

Since appropriations are made to the Coast Guard by type of expenditure, the budget system must provide controls to insure that obligations and expenditures stay within appropriation limits. The activity schedule is a good example of performance budgeting. It groups budgetary data by the type of operational activity and is primarily a tool of operating managers who must carry out these activities. The program budget, on the other hand, is designed to focus attention on the outputs and objectives of the Coast Guard—those objectives it seeks, and the kinds and levels of output it produces.

Program and Financial Plan

Each agency is required to submit as part of the annual budget process a multiyear (usually five years) program and financial plan according to program categories, subdivided into subcategories and program elements. Both financial costs and, wherever possible, measures of proposed program outputs are provided. In most cases the simple output measures contained in the plan are only indicators of more complicated outputs. Since the President must recommend his budget to Congress in terms of the congressionally established appropriation structure, the plan also provides a "crosswalk" that translates program costs classified by output category into individual appropriation requests.

In effect, the program and financial plan is a tabular record of an agency's proposed activities, measured in both physical and financial terms and grouped by output-oriented categories. Originally the program and financial plan was conceived as a five-year planning document, incorporating proposals for program decisions over that five-year period. In early 1967 the program and financial plan was modified for most agencies so that future financial and output data reflected only the consequences of decisions proposed for the subsequent budget.

As a hypothetical case, let us assume that the Federal Aviation Administration proposes in the 1969 budget to initiate procurement of long lead-time equipment for traffic control systems at air terminals (radars, computers, display equipment, and the like). The five-year, time-phased costs of procuring, installing, and operating the system would be included in the agency's program and financial plan. These would be the future costs of current decisions. But if the agency also believed that in 1970 a series of improvements in air navigation facilities would be desirable, the costs and outputs of this project would not be included in the current program and financial plan since a decision need not be made on the matter until the next year's budget. Thus, the program and financial plan is not a planning document in the true sense of the word since the plan does not fully reflect the agency's proposed course of action over the period covered by the plan. There are, in effect, two types of forward plans: The first covers the future budgetary consequences of current decisions—it provides an information system whereby built-in budgetary increases can be estimated, in the aggregate and by individual programs; the second projects the composition of agency programs over an extended period, including the consequences of decisions which will not be taken for several years. Such plans are, by nature, highly tentative and change periodically. But they can be an important, internal management tool through which an agency head may influence the long-range

27

course of his department. The ambiguities and difficulties that accompany the pursuit of long-term planning will be discussed in Chapter 5.

The program and financial plan, as I mentioned earlier, includes a bridge between the program budget and the appropriation structure. From a technical standpoint this is necessary because program decisions have to be translated into specific appropriation requests. But more importantly, it turns out that it is impossible for the department head, the budget director, or the President to make decisions solely on the basis of program categories. In most civilian agencies the individual appropriations have lives of their own. The problems that arise in integrating the PPB system into the political process can be seen from the following example. In the Department of Agriculture there is a program subcategory called "agricultural production capacity," which covers those programs aimed at increasing farm efficiency and productivity.[2] Some of the activities in this subcategory are research efforts, such as control of crop-destroying pests and research into better seed strains. Most of this research is carried on by the Agricultural Research Service, which also conducts equally important research affecting other programs—nutrition and agricultural marketing and distribution, to mention a few.

Appropriations are made directly to the Agricultural Research Service—the administering agency. There is one appropriation for operating expenses and another for facilities construction. The Appropriations Committees are vitally interested in what happens to the Agricultural Research Service as an organiza-

2. As a sidelight on the problems involved, a companion subcategory in the same program is labeled "farm income." This subcategory includes most of the price support programs—whose major objective is to *limit* farm production as a means of raising prices and income.

tional entity. The committees are particularly concerned with the dispensing of operating funds to the hundreds of small agricultural research stations judiciously scattered throughout the country—stations which are often too small to be efficient. They are also interested in the facilities appropriation, both the overall size and the particular location of proposed facilities. Other research in the production capacity program category is carried out through formula grants to university agricultural experiment stations. These grants are administered by the Co-operative State Research Service, a separate organization with a separate appropriation. This service also makes grants for research in program categories other than production capacity. Here, again, a whole new set of interests—well-organized in-terests—affects the appropriation to the Cooperative State Re-search Service. It determines the fate of a particular set of institutions across the country.

The agricultural Extension Service provides another example. The service administers the federal grants-in-aid to the state agri-cultural extension programs. Agricultural extension activities are quite diverse, and in the program or output-oriented budget these activities are assigned to various categories, depending on the particular objective. The appropriations for all of these programs, however, are made to a single organization—the Extension Service. The size and language of that appropria-tion is again a matter of vital concern to the Appropriations Committees and to the well-organized agricultural extension interests, whose influence was felt by the administration several years ago when it tried to substitute direct project grants—determined on "merit"—for a small fraction of the formula grants. The goal of the administration was precisely to direct the extension grants toward specific program objectives, and in par-ticular toward the alleviation of rural poverty. This attempt was defeated on grounds that the administration was seeking to seize control of program content.

Because organizations have a political importance in their own right, it has been impossible to make budget decisions solely on the basis of program categories. The allocation of budget resources cannot be decided solely on the basis of how those resources contribute to program objectives. The implicit effect of budgetary decisions on organizations remains an essential element in the decision process.

These same problems occur in almost every civilian agency. I am not simply making the point that consideration of political values must enter into major decisions on program strategy— that fact is too obvious to need comment. What is significant here is that even at the lowest level of detail, decisions about the effectiveness and efficiency of programs impinge upon the political values—and indeed the very future—of particular groups in society. This aspect of PPB is much more pervasive in most civilian agencies than in the Department of Defense. This is exemplified by the broad general structure of the Department of Defense appropriations compared to the detailed structure of appropriations for the Department of Health, Education, and Welfare.

As a consequence of this fact, PPB has not been characterized by the making of program decisions that are mechanically translated into appropriation requests. Rather, the installation of PPB has led to a parallel and interacting process under which decisions have been based on a joint consideration of program structure and appropriation structure. This should not be considered a downgrading of PPB. It simply reflects that PPB and all it entails can be an important part, but not the whole, of the decision process, no matter what level of detail is being examined.

The Program Memorandum

While the program and financial plan is a tabular record of cost and output consequences of proposed budgetary decisions, the program memorandum provides the strategic and analytical justification for these decisions. Each major program is covered by a program memorandum. Ideally, it summarizes the analytic basis for important policy and budget choices. Since every program area encompasses a multitude of individual program elements, each of which requires some budgetary decisions, the program memorandum is designed to cover only the major issues. Indeed, the number of major issues requiring analysis far exceeds the capacity of existing staffs. In areas where no analytical work has been done, the program memorandum simply identifies major decision proposals and provides a statement of why particular choices are recommended. Thus, the PPB system tries from the start to force an *explicit* statement of broad program strategy as the basis for detailed budget decisions, even where limitations on staff resources make detailed analysis impossible. This is part of the constant attempt to integrate broad policy and program decisions into the budgetary process rather than having the two proceed on separate tracks, with a forced reconciliation at the end.

Special Issues

The program memorandum, to be a useful tool of decision making, cannot incorporate the in-depth analytical studies of program issues, but can only summarize the basic program strategy, and, where relevant, the analysis on which it is based. Each year the Bureau of the Budget and the individual federal agencies jointly agree on a number of program issues for which detailed analytic studies are to be carried out. The results of these studies are themselves the subject of discussion and debate, and form the basis for program memoranda. Often these studies relate to issues that cut across many program categories—federal policy in distributing research grants among various kinds of institutions, the role of federal hospitals in improving hospital design and management, criteria for setting user charges in federal recreation areas, and so forth.

Misconceptions about PPB

Several misconceptions surround PPB and its objectives. To many people, the use of program or output-oriented categories in the budgetary process is the chief element and distinguishing characteristic of PPB. The program grouping of budgetary data is, indeed, a most important aid in the analytic decision-making process, since program budgets, when properly conceived, almost force the decision maker to think in output terms. But other elements of PPB are equally, if not more, important.

Another misconception is that there is a single "ideal" program structure. Program structures are not immutable and should be changed as circumstances change. Moreover, for the analysis of certain problems several crosscutting sets of program categories are needed. A program structure that provides across-the-board information on federal support for basic research, or on all federal funds flowing to universities, is quite useful for some purposes. But the components of these programs are also included in the mission-oriented programs of different agencies. For some purposes veterans' housing programs are viewed as veterans' benefits; for others this program must be combined with other housing programs. Program structures, therefore, need be neither unidimensional nor immutable. While the program structure is an important part of PPB, it is by no means the be-all and end-all of the system.

The effectiveness of PPB does not depend on reorganizing operating units to conform to program categories, as is often claimed. In fact, this would be harmful in some cases and impossible in others. Organizations are characterized, chiefly, by the type of operations they carry out. For efficient management this is an appropriate organizational criterion. But each organization usually contributes to several different kinds of output. To split the Agricultural Research Service into five or six components and to recombine one of those components with parts of the Soil Conservation Service just because they both contribute to raising farm productivity makes little managerial sense.

One of the most important aspects of the whole PPB system—and the one that still causes a good deal of trouble—is its relationship to the annual budget cycle within the executive. Budgetary decisions are crowded into the months of October through December. There is literally no time for extended analysis of program proposals. More important, the detailed preparation of budget requests in the thousands of bureaus, offices, and field establishments of the federal government must begin much earlier than the October–December period. Analytic studies, initial drafts of program memoranda, and basic outlines of proposed financial plans should be available by midsummer if they are to have a meaningful impact on subsequent budget formulation. Ideally, a series of major decisions would be ready in midsummer, on the basis of which detailed budgetary requests could be written. Realistically, this is impossible. No President, budget director, or agency head is likely to make decisions about the size of the poverty budget, the new housing program, or the pace of the postlunar landing effort until the overall size of the budget and the expected shape of future economic conditions are known. This information is not available in midsummer. But the availability of the results of special studies and of draft program memoranda earlier in the budget cycle are critical to the success of the system. These documents, even in draft form, can be a vehicle for isolating differences in major issues, for discovering what additional information is required, and, most important, for putting the agency head's perspective on the detailed budget requests that his subordinates send to him. For numerous reasons, however, a proper time cycle has not yet been established. In too many cases, program memoranda and special studies are available only *after* the subordinate units of the agency have submitted their budget requests to the secretary. As a consequence, they often come too late to have any impact on those requests and lose some of their effectiveness as a vehicle for critical discussion of alternative courses of action and for decisions on overall program strategy.

This, then, is the basic nature of the planning, programming, and budgeting system as it is being developed and applied in the civilian agencies of the federal government. In one sense, it is a systematic organization of the third step in the budgetary reform which began more than fifty years ago: financial control, managerial efficiency, and, now, strategic planning. But its basic aims are substantially different from those of the preceding steps. It brings both the budgetary process and the analytic problem-solving approach into the specification of objectives and the selection of alternatives among programs, and these are the very essence of the political process. Although PPB does not seek to replace the political decision-making process, it will—if successful—modify that process. And, equally, it must adapt itself to the essentially political nature of program decision making.

3 Muddling Through: An Alternative View of the Decision Process

The planning, programming, and budgeting system as it is applied in civilian agencies of the federal government differs substantially from earlier improvements in the budgetary process insofar as it impinges, at virtually every level of detail, directly on the political process. PPB attempts to influence the choice of both ends and means with a problem-solving approach—that is, it emphasizes analytical criteria of effectiveness and efficiency rather than political criteria of consensus; it deliberately seeks to force examination of a wider range of alternatives than those typically dealt with in the political process; it stresses long-run planning rather than "muddling through."

In the political science and public administration literature of the past decade, there has developed a sophisticated and realistic theory of the political decision-making process which implicitly, and in a few cases explicitly, seems to raise very fundamental criticisms of PPB. It is primarily associated with Charles E. Lindblom, who has developed it in a series of books and articles over the past ten years or more.[1] An outline of this theory and a comparison of its approach to decision making with that incorporated in PPB will provide a useful basis for subsequent examination of how PPB can realistically fit into and support the political process by which decisions are reached.

The fate of anyone who develops a well-articulated theory is to watch helplessly as others shamelessly oversimplify its subtle shadings in an attempt to summarize and compress. Here, the contrast between Lindblom's approach and PPB will deliber-

1. Charles E. Lindblom, "The Science of 'Muddling Through,'" *Public Administration Review*, Vol. XIX, No. 2 (Spring 1959), pp. 79–88; "Decision-Making in Taxation and Expenditures," in National Bureau of Economic Research, *Public Finances: Needs, Sources, and Utilization* (Princeton University Press for NBER, 1961); David Braybrooke and Charles Lindblom, *A Strategy of Decision: Policy Evaluation as a Social Process* (Macmillan, 1963); and Charles Lindblom, *The Intelligence of Democracy* (Macmillan, 1965).

ately be sharpened in order to stress the important points which need to be made. Consequently, I cannot guarantee that Mr. Lindblom and his associates would be willing to claim parentage for what is described. However, I think my outline captures the spirit of their approach.

The Lindblom theory of the decision process implicitly attacks the PPB approach on the following grounds.

First, PPB is unrealistic. The actual decision-making process is not suited to the problem-solving approach. Therefore, PPB will wreck itself upon the rocks of reality.

Second, not only is PPB incompatible with the realities of politics, it would not represent a desirable decision system even if it were politically acceptable. In a free political society, the problem-solving approach does not usually arrive at "good" decisions. It attempts, at too many points, to substitute efficiency criteria for the more meaningful criterion of achieving consensus through adjustment of conflicting values. And by its emphasis on the explicit statement of ends and objectives PPB can intensify unproductive ideological debate.

Third, the analytic approach associated with PPB—in particular its attempt to specify and measure ends, to separate means from ends, and to examine a wide range of alternatives— is unattainable and undesirable when applied to social and institutional problems.

Before elaborating on the Lindblom approach it is important to note two points. First, Lindblom's writings preceded the installation of PPB in the civilian agencies of the federal government. At no point does he explicitly mention PPB. Second, and more important, Lindblom's primary concern was to establish the limits of the comprehensive problem-solving approach as a means of arriving at decisions that deal with complex and highly political matters. I will examine the *apparent* conflict between

36

PPB on the one hand and the political bargaining process on the other within the framework of Lindblom's analysis. As a result of this approach, the contrast between Lindblom's emphasis on the limitations of analysis and my emphasis on pushing out those limits appears sharper than it really is. But just as I would not deny that there are limits to the application of PPB, so Lindblom would not deny that there is a role for PPB and that the limits he describes can be pushed out.[2] Indeed, the aim of this book is not to sharpen the differences between the political bargaining approach and the analytical approach to decision making, but rather to find a partial synthesis between the two, at least in the sense of defining the appropriate role of each. The relatively sharp contrast between the two decision techniques drawn (or perhaps "overdrawn") in this chapter is a necessary first step toward this goal.

Ends and Means

Central to the Lindblom approach is its emphasis on the difficulty of specifying the ends or objectives of public programs and the impossibility of separating ends from means.

We can start with the obvious proposition that various social ends or values are in conflict with each other. I am not speaking of opportunity costs in the allocation of resources—with a limited budget the cost of having more of one good is accepting less of another. There is a deeper conflict of values associated with most choices.[3] The more ambitious our goals in terms of

2. Lindblom explicitly makes this point in a letter to me, July 5, 1968.

3. This proposition does not apply when the existing situation constitutes an "inferior" solution—that is, when some change can be made that allows us to have more of one value without a sacrifice of others. Whether "most" choices involve conflicts of values depends on whether in "most" situations we are living with inferior solutions.

full employment, the more we must sacrifice goals of price stability and balance-of-payments equilibrium. Programs that seek to raise farm prices and incomes conflict with the objective of lower consumer prices. The goal of reducing traffic accidents conflicts with the desire for rapid transportation and widespread car ownership. The goal of efficient urban transportation often conflicts with aesthetic values and values associated with displacing low-income residents. Altruistic values are an important part of the political process, and professional cynics are unrealistic in denying their existence. Nevertheless, altruistic values conflict among themselves as well as with self-interest values.

Not only do our social ends or values conflict, but being quite subtle and complex, they are exceedingly difficult to specify. We simply cannot determine in the abstract our ends or values and the intensity with which we hold them. *We discover our objectives and the intensity that we assign to them only in the process of considering particular programs or policies.* We articulate "ends" as we evaluate "means."

Consider the examples of conflicting values cited above. No one can specify in advance the weight he attaches to traffic safety versus rapid transportation except when considering a specific traffic safety program and evaluating its particular impact on the transportation system. We all subscribe to both the goals of ending poverty and of preserving work incentives. But we do not have an abstract social welfare function that predetermines our tradeoffs between these two goals and that can be applied toward making a choice in any given situation. Yet we can make a decision about a particular piece of social welfare legislation that sets certain specific income limits on welfare payments and exempts a specified portion of earned income from that limit. We all are interested in reducing the crime rate, and also in preserving individual rights, but we can handle problems of the tradeoff between the two only when considering a concrete program which affects both these goals.

In brief, our values or goals become meaningful only when the means to achieve them are examined. The reason for this is twofold: First, since our values and the weights attached to them are extremely subtle and complex, no attempt to articulate them in advance will encompass all their shadings and intensities. But we can handle the subset of those shadings and intensities that are raised by a particular policy issue. Second, any given course of action usually involves many different values. In the case of the unemployment-inflation tradeoff, we might conceivably specify in advance the tradeoff function that reflects our value system. But any particular fiscal policy will involve other values besides these two. We may be especially concerned, at a particular moment, about the impact of unemployment on summer riots, or on depressed economic areas. We may not like the income distribution consequences of a given tax measure designed to achieve a desired unemployment-inflation mix, or the consequences of an expenditure cut on federal social programs. But the tradeoff we might have chosen, considering only the objectives of unemployment and inflation, may not be acceptable when the particular policy actions affect many other values. And these various values cannot, usually, be measured in terms that allow one to be directly compared with others—that is, weights cannot be assigned to them. Conceptually this kind of problem can be handled in terms of a multidimensional social welfare function. In practice, however, there are so many "dimensions" to most public programs that there is no possibility of determining, in the abstract, multidimensional tradeoff functions among different, usually noncommensurable, values.

The detailed legislative specifications and appropriation structures for most social programs stem from the fact that the particular provisions of a public program usually impinge upon a number of political values. What may appear to the analyst as a technical means to affect one generally accepted objective usually has subsidiary implications for many other objectives about which there is much less agreement. The obvious analogy is with consumer preference theory. Our preference function is revealed to us only by the act of making a particular choice among goods, and then only in the region of the function immediately surrounding the choice point.

Not only do we indicate our objectives through the consideration of particular means to achieve them, but we actually discover new objectives at the same time. For example, imagine a world in which there were no Polaris missiles, or similar systems, but one in which multiple independently targeted reentry vehicles (MIRVs) of large yield and great accuracy were a reality. It would then be impossible to provide a strategic force that could survive an enemy's first strike; every attempt to do so, for example, by adding numbers of hardened missiles, could be offset, at a fraction of the cost, by the enemy adding MIRVs to his force. In such a world I doubt whether the current strategic deterrence objective of "assured destruction capacity"[4] could have been conceived. The existence of large bodies of oil-yielding shale and the necessity to develop a policy for their exploitation has generated policy studies that may well lead to the formulation of objectives concerning U.S. energy policy which might otherwise never have been articulated. Senator Richard B. Russell opposed the Defense Department's request

4. Assured destruction capacity, as an objective for U.S. strategic retaliatory forces, requires that those forces always be sufficient to absorb an enemy's first strike and survive with sufficient capability to inflict irreparable damage on the enemy.

for authorization of the fast deployment logistics ships (FDLs), not on grounds of cost or effectiveness, but because—according to him—they would provide an excessively easy means of intervening militarily in limited wars. Here is a significant objective—the limitation of our military fast response capability—which, I am convinced, was not part of Senator Russell's social welfare function. It evolved, in all probability, during consideration of the specifics of a particular program.

Our ends or values are also hierarchical in nature. Most objectives are valued because they help achieve some higher values, which become more difficult to articulate the further up the scale we go. Ends are simply means to higher ends. Price stability is an objective of public policy because, among other reasons, it affects the distribution of income and the efficiency of forward business planning. We use the grant-in-aid approach in most new social programs partly because it tends to preserve the powers of state and local governments in a federal system. We value this system because it is decentralized, which we value in turn for the sake of political freedom and diversity.

The dual fact that we discover our values while considering the means to achieve them and that values are hierarchical in nature results in a continual change and evolution of our objectives. Experience constantly teaches us that some of our values have less of a connection than we thought with the achievement of higher values. Federal aid to elementary and secondary education was vigorously opposed by many conservatives on grounds that it would lead to a federalized school system. A few years after passage of the Elementary and Secondary Education Act of 1965, this element of opposition has virtually disappeared. The presumed connection between the subordinate goal of financial independence for local school systems and the higher goal of policy independence has been shown by experience not

41

to be as strong as originally thought. Moreover, the constant change in the availability of new instruments of social policy, and the growth of income with which to finance their application, leads to a steady shift and expansion of our social values. The means and resources generate the values and the objectives.

In short, ends are closely intertwined with means, are subtle, complex, constantly being discovered, and are usually in conflict with one another. Moreover, the most obvious fact of political life is that individuals and groups differ widely from each other in the values they hold and the intensity with which they hold those values. If the articulation of a multidimensional set of objectives is difficult for a single individual or group, it is infinitely more difficult for the body politic. Value conflicts arise from the immediate self-interest of various groups—depletion allowances, the location of public works projects, farm and maritime subsidies—and from conflicts over more general values, which stem from long-term self-interest—the power of federal versus the state and local governments, the overall level of federal expenditures and revenues. Other conflicts arise because different groups have quite different visions, in an altruistic sense, of the "good society."

In the Lindblom view values and means are so closely intertwined, policy decisions affect so many different values, and there is such a wide network of conflicts over values that decisions about public programs, even at a relatively low level of detail, are saturated with value choices. Technically, maximizing a known social welfare function subject to a given set of production functions and resource constraints does not fit political reality.

The Consequences of Policy Decisions

In addition to the difficulty of establishing ends apart from means, the Lindblom school lays great stress on the inherent difficulties in predicting the consequences of any particular programmatic means on the wide range of ends or values that exist. In different terminology, the difficulties associated with specifying a social welfare function are compounded by the difficulty in establishing production functions. The more important the policy measure under consideration, the more difficult the problem of predicting its consequences.

In 1962 President John F. Kennedy proposed removing from the Interstate Commerce Commission authority to establish minimum rates on certain classes of freight carried by railroads. The principal immediate effect of this "minimum rate bill" would have been to increase competition between the railroads, on the one hand, and trucks and barge lines, on the other. The administration expected, and received, opposition from the trucking and barge lines. But the death-blow to the bill more probably came from opposition from local interests and port authorities scattered through the country. The existing location of many industries is heavily dependent on the structure of freight rates. Any change in those freight rates could produce changes in comparative advantages in ways that are hard to predict for thousands of communities and industries. It proved to be impossible to determine, in advance, what the impact of the bill would be on industrial location. But uncertainty and the threat of unknown consequences played a major role in killing the bill.

Who could have forecast the diverse impact on local political structures of the language in the original antipoverty bill relating to the "participation of the poor" in the decision structure of community action agencies? Who can now predict the consequences of the new model cities program on social structures, political power, integration, and all the other relevant values in the many urban areas involved? The 41,000 mile interstate highway program, inaugurated in the mid-1950s, has had consequences for almost every aspect of American life—speedier intercity transportation being only one of the effects. The comparative advantage of industrial locations on the outer fringes of urban areas has been sharply increased; the tax structure of metropolitan areas has been significantly affected; the recreation habits of the population have been altered, and the demand for national parks dramatically increased. The chain of consequences was so wide as to defy prediction at the time the program was launched—and indeed its ramifications defy ex post analysis. G. L. S. Shackle, in his 1966 presidential address to the Royal Economic Society aptly stated the problem:

Is the nature of things, the so-called human predicament, such that we face an endless examination in arithmetic, each hour presenting its sum, and the subsequent hours or years marking our answer right or wrong? If so, policy-making is problem solving, there is an algebra of business which only needs to be supplied with a sufficiency of information to guarantee success. Or is the logic of things such that no such sufficiency of information can ever exist? Is policy-making, by necessity, an originative art? Art is the manipulation of constraints.... Art is not arbitrary, unconstrained caprice. But the required knowledge may be knowledge of what *can* be done rather than what *must* be done.[5]

Uncertainty about the performance of hardware systems can be substantially reduced with additional information, and the consequences of uncertainty in terms of the assigned task of the system can be systematically examined by techniques such as

5. G. L. S. Shackle, "Policy, Poetry and Success," *Economic Journal*, Vol. LXXVI, No. 304 (December 1966), pp. 755–56 (italics supplied).

sensitivity analysis. However, it is much more difficult to reduce uncertainty over the effects of federal programs on social and institutional behavior. And the consequences of uncertainty for decision making are similarly more difficult to unravel. Difficult as it is to predict the output of a major missile system in terms of assured destruction capacity, it is substantially easier to analyze than, say, the impact of the model cities program on the social and institutional structure of the ghetto. Of course, the ultimate objective of a strategic missile system is its effect on the behavior of Soviet and Chinese decision makers, and this is no easier to predict than the consequences of a model cities program. In terms of *ultimate* objectives or values, that observation is correct. Insofar as missile systems and space programs have, as objectives, an influence on men's minds, their ultimate output is as hard to predict as that of any social program. But the difference between the analysis of hardware systems and social programs is that the *proximate* consequences of the social programs are substantially less susceptible to prediction than are those of hardware programs. This inherent limitation of the human mind to analyze the full sweep of the social and institutional consequences of major programs is a key element in the Lindblom approach.

Another aspect of the decision process, heavily stressed by Aaron Wildavsky,[6] relates to the political costs of political decisions. There are political opportunity costs to any decision, just as real as the economic opportunity costs. Because values conflict among different groups and among themselves, securing the agreement necessary to pursue one line of action most often reduces the opportunity to pursue other lines of action. This is

6. Aaron Wildavsky, "The Political Economy of Efficiency: Cost-Benefit Analysis, Systems Analysis, and Program Budgeting," *Public Administration Review*, Vol. XXVI, No. 4 (December 1966), pp. 292–310.

a different kind of opportunity cost. Securing the support of one particular bloc in Congress for passage of, say, an education bill, may require commitments out of a limited pool of appointment patronage, or that hostages may be given the bloc in terms of support for or opposition to other measures. An education bill may, for example, be associated with a series of public works projects. Another cost incurred in passing one bill may be the alienation of support for other bills. A civil rights bill may "cost" a housing bill. To take another hypothetical example, an administration might have the votes to override opposition and sharply increase the repayment formula on irrigation projects—requiring irrigators to pay back a higher proportion of project costs. But irrigation appears absolutely vital to a particular group of congressmen. Overriding their "veto" on irrigation policy may well insure their opposition to other decisions on which they might have been neutral or mildly favorable. These considerations not only enter the relations between the executive and the Congress, but also affect the internal decision process within the executive, which also represents a coalition of divergent interests.

More generally, because most programs have consequences for a wide range of values about which there are sharply divided views, it is impossible for any political leader to consider a single program decision in isolation. The effect of any one decision on a whole system of decisions must be taken into account. Beyond the more immediate opportunity costs of decisions—the cost of one decision in terms of others—there are opportunity costs for the decision process as a whole. To secure the enactment of a positive program of actions, a consensus or coalition must be put together which bridges a wide divergence of values. That consensus or coalition is usually elastic, but not infinitely so. Decisions that put a radical strain on the consensus may take their toll not only on individual future decisions but on the whole process. The consensus may be destroyed, the coalition fragmented, the process disrupted. These costs dictate a set of efficiency criteria for political decisions equally as real and valid as the resource costs which lead to the efficiency criteria of systematic analysis.[7]

The Science of Muddling Through

All the foregoing considerations indicate a particular type of decision process that seems, at first glance, quite different from the rational problem-solving approach associated with PPB. This decision process is presented by Lindblom and others both as a description of reality and as a prescription for "good" decisions.

Minimizing Debate about Values

The first rule of the successful political process is, "Don't force a specification of goals or ends." Debate over objectives should be minimized partly because ends and means are inseparable. More important, the necessary agreement on particular policies can often be secured among individuals or groups who hold quite divergent ends.

The Elementary and Secondary Education Act of 1965 broke

7. The analogy between political opportunity costs and economic opportunity costs can be pushed still further. An economic system is judged not only for efficiency in the static sense—that is, allocating resources efficiently toward satisfying the economic demands of its members, given the existing set of production functions—but also for efficiency in the dynamic sense—that is, expanding the level of output by discovering and using new production functions. Similarly, an effective political leader not only maximizes what he can achieve from the existing constellation of political forces, but also finds means of changing that constellation of forces to make possible a wider range of potential achievements.

new ground in terms of federal aid to education. It was enacted precisely because it was constructed to attract the support of three groups, each with quite different ends in view. Some saw it as the beginning of a large program of federal aid to public education. The parochial school interests saw it as the first step in providing, albeit indirectly, financial assistance for parochial school children. The third group saw it as an antipoverty measure, since the distribution formula for Title I of the bill—containing the largest part of the funds—is based on the number of poor children in each school district. Two other crosscutting values were taken care of in the bill: Title I provided formula grants to school districts over which the federal government had little control. Title III, on the other hand, provided individual federal project grants for specific innovative programs.[8] If there had been any attempt to secure advance agreement on a set of long-run objectives, important elements of support for the bill would have been lost, and its defeat assured.

Another example is the wheat price-support program enacted in 1964. The earlier proposed program was built around mandatory federal controls over wheat acreage, aimed at reducing supply and maintaining income. The controls would have applied to all wheat farmers. But to become effective the law required a favorable vote from wheat farmers, in a referendum, on the establishment of acreage controls. The referendum resulted in a negative vote. The consequent lack of any wheat program would have led to a drastic fall in wheat prices and incomes. The new program, developed in response to this situation, provided for direct federal payments to farmers who agreed "voluntarily" to reduce their wheat acreage. This program

8. Subsequently, in the "Green" amendments of 1967, the federal government's selection among project applicants was sharply reduced in favor of state boards of education.

secured the support of two quite distinct groups. One group sought a subsidy program acceptable to farmers that would avoid a sharp fall in wheat prices during an election year. The other group saw in the direct payment scheme the possibility, at some future time, of placing a limit on the subsidies paid to high-income farmers. (Under the older programs, it was technically impossible to tailor the benefits to the income of the farmer.) The two groups had diametrically opposite objectives. Yet both were able to agree on the same program—precisely because ultimate goals and objectives were not forced into the debate.

Income distribution is another example. Ideally, the nation should agree on a "desired" distribution of income, and adjust tax rates and program subsidies on the basis of that decision. But clearly the attempt would be disastrous. No agreement could be reached on a global specification. But we can and do agree on specific pieces of legislation that have fairly predictable consequences for income distribution.

In the political world depicted by Lindblom, specification of objectives is not only intellectually difficult but pragmatically objectionable. Ideological dispute accomplishes nothing substantial but it blocks pragmatic agreement among diverse interests on specific measures. A decision technique that emphasizes the precise and careful statement of objectives can, under this view of political reality, prove positively harmful.

Incrementalism

The second feature of a desirable decision process, in the theory we are examining, is its incremental nature. Because political decision costs tend to mount the more the decisions conflict with the values held by important groups, and because our ability to foresee the full social consequences of any program

49

change is so limited, movement toward objectives should proceed by small steps.

Radical actions take us beyond the realm of reasonable foresight. We make progress by sequential steps, correcting and adjusting for unforeseen consequences as we go. The whole route is not planned in advance. This form of planning by small increments has been called "Lewis and Clark" planning as opposed to "Cook's tour" planning.[9] Both goals and steps toward the goals should be modest. In most cases we can neither specify nor get agreement upon more radical goals—goals that require large departures from present experience. Moreover, since the consequences of social programs are so complex and far reaching, it is difficult to predict whether any major departure from current policies will move us toward a particular goal and virtually impossible to foresee the consequences of our actions on other values or goals. According to this theory, inertia of government bureaus, which so limits the flexibility and freedom of action of cabinet secretaries and Presidents, reflects not merely bureaucratic caution but the built-in wisdom of making progress by small steps.

Political incrementalism has its analogue in analytic incrementalism. It does not pay, in analyzing a federal program or any proposed course of political action, to scan a wide range of fundamentally differing alternatives. Analysis should be confined to a relatively small number of alternatives, differing not too drastically from current policies or programs. While evaluating alternatives, only a few of the major and more immediate consequences of proposed actions should be examined. Attempts to predict the full range of consequences of actions mislead policy

9. James R. Schlesinger, "Organizational Structures and Planning," in Roland N. McKean (ed.), *Issues in Defense Economics* (Columbia University Press for National Bureau of Economic Research, 1967).

makers by giving the appearance of more certainty than can possibly be had. Incrementalism urges modest goals for analysis and policy. For longer-term planning it substitutes policy making by sequential trial and error.

The Advocacy Process

Another major element in the Lindblom approach is the great emphasis placed on the advocacy process as a means of reaching decisions. The individual analyst or analytic staff cannot possibly trace the consequences of policy decisions for the wide range of values that are important to various groups in society. But if the decision process is so structured that advocates of every significantly affected interest have a voice in policy making, then self-interest will insure that each advocate traces out, and vigorously presents, the consequences of any action for the value or values he represents.

In actual practice the political process is structured to give wide scope to this advocacy process. It is impossible to make a policy proposal in Washington without stirring up an incredible array of interest groups, each joining in the debate and uncovering real or alleged relationships between the proposed policy and its own interests—relationships that the policy proponents may never have dreamed existed. There are thousands of individuals whose full-time occupation is the careful examination of proposed legislation or executive actions, seeking to discover implications for the interests of the groups they represent.

The committee system of the Congress and the executive branch are both structured to promote this advocacy process. Few policies are decided on without the participation of many federal agencies in addition to the one that has primary responsibility. The decision process within the executive branch is geared to maximize rather than minimize policy debate among agencies.

Of equal importance is the pervasive web of relationships between the executive and the Congress. There are long-standing channels between federal bureaus and congressional subcommittees, along which information and influence pass as cabinet secretaries come and go. The decision process is fragmented and widely distributed, with many centers of advocacy brought to bear on almost every significant decision.

Decisions are reached, therefore, through an advocacy or bargaining process in a highly pluralistic decentralized system. In this way a mutual adjustment of widely differing values is achieved, not by ideological agreement on specified ends but by pragmatic agreement on particular means. Progress in this system (presumably toward the "good," the "true," and the "beautiful") is made by trial and error, through successive approximations, with both ends and means being continually modified by increments.

This approach is pragmatic and meliorative rather than radical and idealistic. It follows the spirit of the common law rather than the Napoleonic code, emphasizing muddling through rather than long-term planning. It stresses process rather than substantive criteria. A "good" decision is one which gains consensus rather than one which meets outside criteria of efficiency or effectiveness. The political decision process has evolved in this direction because it is a successful means of coping, in a reasonably free society, with the reconciliation of divergent interests and values and the inherent limitations of the human mind to predict the consequences of social policies.

This outline of the decision process is, in many respects, a reasonably accurate description of the existing state of affairs.

Many of its normative prescriptions are attractive. At the same time it appears, at least on first glance, to be in sharp contrast with the outlook and methodology underlying the planning, programming, and budgeting system. Let me now turn to an examination of the role of PPB in the context of this decision model.

4 The Role of Analysis in Political Decisions

In seeking to discover a synthesis between the political and the analytic approach to policy making it is useful to distinguish between the *analysis* of programs and the PPB *system* which integrates that analysis with budgetary decisions. This chapter examines the role of analysis, while the subsequent chapter looks at the system.

Relating Political Values to Program Decisions

[Two propositions are essential to the discussion. First, participants in the decision process cannot evaluate the characteristics of a particular program proposal directly in terms of political values. If we think of program characteristics or specifications as inputs, those inputs must be translated into outputs or consequences before the program can be evaluated. The linkage runs from inputs to outputs to values.] If I place a high value on reducing infant mortality, I still cannot decide about a particular program for maternal or infant care without first knowing what the particular specifications of various alternative proposals yield in terms of a concrete reduction in the infant mortality rate. I may value compensatory education in the urban ghetto as a desirable output but it is an insufficient basis for evaluating a particular grant-in-aid program to central city school districts. I must know, as a minimum, the extent to which the federal program increases the resources going into the ghetto school systems (instead of merely substituting for state and local resources).

[In a sense we work "downward" from general values by specifying in operationally meaningful terms the particular outputs that are called for by those values. We work "upward" from program inputs by determining the outputs that they produce. Outputs are the link between values at one end of the spectrum and detailed program specifications or inputs at the other.] Val-

55

ues cannot be *directly* connected with inputs. Consequently, participants in the decision process must have some knowledge of the social production functions that translate program specifications (inputs) into program consequences (outputs). Otherwise the advocacy and bargaining process cannot produce a meaningful translation of political values into specific decisions.

This proposition is an analogue to consumer preference theory. Resource inputs—labor and capital—are not directly evaluated in terms of consumer preference functions, but only through an imputation process which assumes knowledge of the production functions that translate inputs into outputs. It is the latter, not the former, that enters directly into consumer preferences. The political bargaining process can evaluate and make reasonably meaningful decisions about program specifications only if those specifications can be translated into program outputs. Quite apart, for the moment, from the specification of objectives, we need to know the social production functions of particular programs.[1]

The second proposition is that the need for careful analysis of the production functions of federal programs has increased sharply in recent years. The role of the federal government has significantly expanded in areas where the relationship between inputs and outputs is exceedingly complex and incapable of being grasped by intuition, rule of thumb, or reliance on past experience.

As I pointed out earlier, the federal budget for civilian programs—apart from interest on the public debt, veterans' benefits,

1. I use the term *social* production functions simply to emphasize that many of the domestic programs of the federal government do not deal with the transformation of resource inputs into commodities, where the nature of the production function is heavily conditioned by engineering and technological considerations. Rather the production functions are shaped by institutional and behavioral characteristics.

and the Post Office—has risen from less than 1 percent of the GNP in the 1920s to 5 percent in the immediate postwar period to almost 10 percent at the present time. In the last four years alone (fiscal 1965 to fiscal 1969) federal outlays on education rose from $5 billion to over $11 billion and federal funds for health programs from $5.5 billion to more than $15 billion. In 1962 there were no federal manpower training or work experience programs while in 1969 1.3 million people will be involved in federally financed training or work experience programs.

Social Production Functions

One major characteristic of most of the newer programs—in contrast to more traditional federal activities—is a highly complex set of relationships between inputs and outputs.

For example, federal elementary and secondary education programs primarily consist of grants-in-aid to state and local governments. It is essential to know whether federal funds are additive to or simply substitutes for state and local education funds. As a substitute for state and local funds, federal aid to education does not increase the resources going into education, but is simply a form of general financial assistance to state and local governments. To the extent that federal funds are additive, they increase resource inputs. Assuming the federal program to be additive, what particular resources does it add, and what consequences do those additional resources have on various measures of educational achievement? Alternative programs will produce different results in terms of additivity and the mix of resource inputs. We cannot choose among them, in order to achieve a particular set of objectives, until we know what those differences are.

The federal water pollution control program raises exceedingly

57

complex questions concerning the relation between program inputs and outputs. Both federal and state governments set and enforce standards of water quality. The federal government makes grants to local governments for waste treatment facilities. Since both the pollution effluents and the pollution control efforts of one community in a river basin have substantial effects on other communities, a meaningful program of standards, controls, and facilities cannot be conceived or executed community by community, but must take into account whole river basins. The long-term effectiveness of pollution control measures will be substantially shaped by the system of user charges designed to pay for the cost of pollution control facilities. Because the facilities built by an upstream community will reduce the pollution faced by a downstream community, user charges must be calculated and assessed in terms of these intercommunity effects. And, in the case of pollution, there are significant value conflicts, since the stringency of controls and the assessment of user charges can substantially influence the location of industry. Meaningful bargaining and advocacy about federal pollution control programs can scarcely proceed without some knowledge of the production functions that relate the characteristics of alternative federal programs to particular pollution control outputs. And, in this case, it takes quite sophisticated analysis to yield information about the production functions.

Programs dealing with maternal and child health care have similarly complex production functions. The United States—despite its standard of living—ranks thirteenth in the world in terms of infant mortality, and also rates high in terms of chronic handicapping conditions in children. If the Swedish infant mortality rate had applied in the United States, there would have been 43,000 fewer infant deaths in 1964 than actually occurred. Excessive infant mortality rates, however, are highly concentrated by area and income grouping. For example, in 1964, the rate for the United States as a whole was 24.8 per 1,000 live births. But 90 percent of the counties had rates of 18.3 or less. Moreover, one-fourth of the excess infant deaths (that is, the excess over the tenth percentile rate) occurred in only 21 out of the 3,130 counties in the United States.

In 1966, the Department of Health, Education, and Welfare undertook a comparative study of alternative maternal and child health care programs. As a result of this study it was possible to determine a rough specification of the production functions for each of the various alternatives, that is, the number of infant deaths and chronic handicapping conditions expected to be pre-- vented under different program structures. The study also considered relevant production constraints—in particular the availability of pediatricians and obstetricians. With this analysis completed, it became possible to discuss the cost and feasibility of achieving various goals. As a result of this study, a specific program including early case findings, periodic medical treatment, and screening of poor children was recommended in 1967, and subsequently enacted. Because of the program's high cost effectiveness it was assigned substantial additional funds in a tight 1969 budget.

[To an increasing extent, particularly as the federal government's social programs expand, knowledge of even the immediate consequences of program specifications requires systematic analysis. It cannot be gained from intuition or reliance on past experience—there is little past experience. The advocacy process, bringing different values and points of view to play on a policy question, is of little use without some knowledge of the relationship between program inputs and outputs.]

Unfortunately, it is common in the bargaining over new programs or the expansion of existing ones for participants to disagree sharply about the output consequences of program inputs. Too often the debate proceeds without either side presenting meaningful evidence or analysis on the specific outputs the program will produce. Supporters of a proposal, for example, often assume that if the program objective is laudatory, the program should be adopted. "You're either for more resources for education or against it."

[Production functions cannot be determined simply by quizzing the technical expert] that is, relying solely on physicians to evaluate health programs or engineers to design pollution control programs. [We are dealing with complicated systems in which institutional, economic, and technical factors interact with each other. Analysis of production functions in most public programs, therefore, must take a systematic approach. It cannot be confined to technical considerations.]

Analysis is also important in program evaluation. Prototypes of social programs, unlike hardware systems, cannot be evaluated and tested in the laboratory or wind tunnel. In our present state of knowledge it is often difficult to predict with any degree of certainty the specific performance of proposed social programs. In such cases the wide range of uncertainty about the relationship between inputs and outputs can be reduced through either ex post evaluation of operating programs or the design and evaluation of demonstration projects. Unfortunately, however, too few programs are routinely subjected to an evaluation of results. Indeed, it is not uncommon for programs of an avowedly experimental nature to be inaugurated with no provision for a systematic evaluation of performance. [The lack of feedback between program results and the decision process even in the case of so-called experimental programs is one of the weakest links in the budgetary system.]

[The process described by Lindblom, of incremental and sequential policy changes, correcting and adjusting at each step, has long been recognized as a highly effective means of proceeding under conditions of uncertainty. But this Lewis and Clark planning does not obviate the need for systematic analysis. The sequential and remedial procedure assumes that each step helps to reduce uncertainty by producing more knowledge about both the production function and the relevance of program outputs to objectives. But that knowledge is not automatically evident to the policy maker from the programs. The complex systems affecting social and institutional behavior demand that program evaluation must be designed with as much care as the program itself. The tests of program accomplishment must reflect program consequences as they relate to operationally specific objectives. In many cases, evaluation must employ relatively sophisticated statistical techniques to sort out the effects of a particular program from other factors influencing test results.

Progress is being made, albeit slowly and painfully. But the design of useful program evaluation studies is a demanding task, and one that often must be pursued in sequential steps. An example is the evaluation of Title I of the Elementary and Secondary Education Act. This title provides formula grants to school districts based upon the number of school children from poor families. The funds involved are only a small portion of the total state and local funds going into elementary and secondary education, which are themselves increasing each year. It is difficult to distinguish Title I effects from other influences. As an early step in the evaluation process a study was made, in some detail, of achievement test scores of selected grades in the schools of fourteen cities. The scores were taken from tests given just prior to the introduction of Title I and again one year later. Test results in the second year were compared with "expected" results based on prior year scores and deviations were identified. One purpose of such identification was to enable additional analysis of particular resource inputs used in schools with large positive deviations. However, further analysis of the underlying data showed the need for much more intensive work before particular resource inputs could be identified with outputs. In case after case, the distribution of limited educational resources within a school or even within an individual class was highly uneven. For example, a remedial reading teacher having four classes might work with only the lowest 10 percent of the students while the next 10 percent would receive no help at all. One class might receive substantial special services, while the others receive few or none. Comparative scores over time for whole classes do not show the effect of additional resources. HEW is presently working on a design for longitudinal evaluation studies which would enable participating school systems to follow the progress of individual students over a period of time and measure the cumulative impact of different types of educational programs on the students as they move through the school system.

In manpower training programs, two major kinds of program evaluation problems arise. First, the evaluation must differentiate program results by age, sex, race, education, prior work experience, and other characteristics of the trainees. A set of program specifications that appears to be successful—in terms of future jobs and incomes—for white, male, high school graduates with prior work experience is not likely to be appropriate for teenage dropouts in central city ghettoes. Second, and much more difficult, is the follow-up problem. Program success depends not only on the proportion of trainees placed in jobs and on their initial wages, but on the permanence of the improved employment experience. Testing this factor requires, again, longitudinal studies of trainees, which is both time consuming and expensive.

Evaluation of the Head Start program in the Office of Economic Opportunity directly led to a major program change. In 1966, evaluation showed that preschool children participating in Head Start made significant gains compared to nonparticipants, but they were quickly lost in the first year of school unless special efforts for these children were continued. As a result of the evaluation, the 1968 and 1969 budgets requested funds for a Head Start Follow Through program, to provide special educational services for Head Start participants in the early grades of school. But since our knowledge of effective techniques in this area is so limited, the program was explicitly designed as experimental, with sufficient funds to institute and evaluate a wide range of alternative techniques.

[Program evaluation is a means of gaining knowledge retrospectively about production functions in order to improve initial predictions, to modify and adjust program design, and to screen out relatively ineffective alternatives. This last aspect causes difficulties, since those in charge of a particular program have an obvious interest in producing favorable evaluations. There is no automatic way to prevent a bias in structuring evaluation studies and interpreting their results] But there are measures that can at least mitigate this bias, which I shall discuss later.

[We have examined two aspects of the role of systematic analysis in the political decision process. In the case of federal social programs, the analysis of production functions provides the crucial link between program specifications on the one hand and values or objectives on the other. The link is fashioned by relating inputs to outputs. Outputs can, in turn, be evaluated in terms of social values. The advocacy process of reconciling divergent values through consideration of particular program measures cannot proceed meaningfully without some knowledge of this link] And particularly in cases of complex social programs, acquisition of that knowledge requires analysis of a system's character—including the specification and examination of objectives and the design of program alternatives.

In many cases, however, our prior knowledge of production functions is quite limited. Uncertainty of this type puts a great premium on careful postprogram evaluation. Feedback of operating results to program planning is essential. Thus, the design and interpretation of evaluations also requires a form of systematic analysis. Systematic analysis, applied to program evaluation, provides—for complex social programs—the necessary feedback ingredient that justifies the incremental, sequential, Lewis and Clark decision-making process.

General Values and Specific Objectives

So far we have considered one of the links between values and program inputs, that is, the social production function which traces the relationship between program characteristics and social outputs. But the discovery of such production functions, either ex ante or ex post, is only half of the chain. The other necessary link is the translation of general values into specific objectives. An evaluation of program outputs in terms of specific objectives can then complete the connection between general values and particular programs or program alternatives.

In complex public programs, systematic analysis is as much needed in establishing the second link, translating values into specific objectives, as it is in discovering the first link, translating program inputs into social outputs. It is a perfectly valid point that values are discovered not in the abstract but during consideration of specific programs, and that values held by advocates in the political process are generally quite vague and unspecified. These facts of life, however, do not obviate the need for systematic analysis—they strengthen it. Indeed, far from quarreling with the Lindblom thesis that ends and means are closely intertwined, systematic analysis uses this as a central proposition underlying its analytical technique.]Systematic analysis does not simply accept objectives as immutably given and then proceed to seek the most effective or efficient means of achieving these objectives.[One of its major contributions to the complex decision-making process lies precisely in its consideration of both objectives and means, allowing analysis of each to influence the other.]

. . . systems analysis rejects the linear form of analysis from given objectives to an optimal alternative, and instead explores the interaction of ends and means in order to help the decision-maker formulate his objectives for purposes of decision.[2]

[Systems analysis is] a cycle of definition of objectives, design of alternative systems to achieve those objectives, evaluation of the alternatives in terms of their effectiveness and costs, a questioning of the objectives and a questioning of the other assumptions underlying the analysis, the opening of new alternatives, the establishment of new objectives, etc.[3]

[Not only is there a constant *analytical* interaction between objectives and means, but the sophisticated analytical process in a political environment also involves a continuing *communications* interaction between the analyst and the policy maker. Analysis of specific objectives and alternative policy action clarifies initial

2. Clay Thomas Whitehead, "Uses and Limitations of Systems Analysis," P–3683 (processed; Santa Monica, Calif.: RAND Corporation, 1967), p. 91. This monograph, particularly Chapters II through IV, provides a highly perceptive analysis of the relationship between the systems analyst and the policy maker in various kinds of organizations.

3. Alain Enthoven, "Operations Research at the National Policy Level" (unpublished transcript of an address at the Operations Evaluation Group Vicennial Conference, Washington, D.C., May 1962), cited by Whitehead, *ibid.*, p. 44.

value judgments leading to revised value judgments which in turn guide further analysis.]

It would be naive to think of PPB as a system in which the analyst, on his own and without constraints, formulates a set of specific objectives for a federal agency, primarily derived from efficiency criteria. But it is equally naive to think that in areas of tremendous complexity, the pure bargaining process can translate a loosely developed set of general values into meaningful operational objectives.] While it is often strategically and tactically important for participants in the bargaining process to conceal their objectives from their adversaries, it hardly behooves them to conceal them from themselves. Ends, as well as means, need systematic examination and analysis. Careful development and critical analysis of objectives—within the limits of outside value constraints—is a highly fruitful technique for gaining insight into the costs and consequences of existing and proposed programs, and a necessary condition for developing a range of program alternatives.

[In attempting to specify at least the major objectives of existing programs, and the constraints that must be observed in reaching those objectives, questions are automatically raised about the relationship of the existing program to the stated objectives. In turn, these questions can suggest a change in the programs, a change in the constraints, or a change in the objectives—or often some combination of changes in all three.]For example, one of the major program categories in the Federal Aviation Administration (FAA) is to "Provide for Safety and Efficiency in Airspace Utilization," which includes, as subcategories, the provision of aids to navigation, landing aids, en route traffic control, terminal traffic control, and flight information. The principal objective for the subcategory on terminal air traffic control as stated by the FAA is to "provide a national system of terminal air traffic service facilities to efficiently accommodate demand for air traffic services at improved levels of safety and minimum levels of delay."

In considering means of achieving this objective the FAA undertook a special study of alternative approaches for reducing delays in terminal areas, based on an analysis of seven major airports.[4] Joint consideration of the program objectives and the alternative means of achieving those objectives immediately raises a series of questions. First, the stated objective is to provide facilities in order to accommodate demand for air traffic. But demand at what price? Is it the function of government to assure a supply of traffic control services sufficient to handle the quantity of those services that would be demanded at a zero price to the user? Clearly, the quantity of airborne traffic to be handled is a function of the price charged for services provided. If the price is sufficiently low, it may encourage enough traffic to congest any conceivable set of facilities that can be built. Or to put the matter another way, if price is not used to ration traffic, then congestion will—regardless of how far facilities are expanded traffic will grow to the point where it creates enough congestion to discourage further traffic growth.

The price elasticity of demand for air traffic control services may be relatively low in the case of commercial aviation—since the cost of the service per passenger is a relatively small component of total trip costs. But the price elasticity is undoubtedly higher for general aviation (the private plane used for business or pleasure) since costs must be spread over a much smaller number of passengers. Moreover, relatively small changes in traffic generate large changes in average delay times at terminals. The FAA study pointed out that a 10 percent increase in demand for

4. U.S. Department of Transportation, Federal Aviation Administration, "Alternative Approaches for Reducing Delays in Terminal Areas," Staff Study (1967).

runways will often result in a 60 percent increase in average delay times, and a 20 percent increase in demand, a 200 percent rise in average delay. Even with a low-price elasticity of traffic demand, therefore, changes in price should generate significant changes in average delays. Safety requirements are not at issue here, since regulations could be introduced that would limit the traffic to the safe capacity of the particular facilities available. The ensuing delays in arrivals and departures would, naturally, be costly. The real question is whether facilities should be provided (indeed can be provided) to reduce to a minimum the delay costs that accompany the volume of traffic generated at a zero price.

Probing further, at the airports studied typical peak hour delays were ten times the overall average delay. User charges for terminal air traffic services based on the "congestion" principle—that is, charges that vary positively with the degree of congestion—would tend to spread traffic more evenly throughout the day and substantially raise the annual volume of traffic that could be handled by any given set of facilities. There are difficult administrative questions involved in levying congestion charges, since the federal government provides traffic control services while the airports are owned and operated by local communities or authorities. The costs of reducing delays fall on both. However, these are not insuperable problems.

Charging a price for the delay-reducing services would have two results: First, it would ration the volume of services to the level at which benefits to the traveler equaled the incremental cost of providing the services, including delay costs imposed on other travelers; and second, it would levy the cost upon the traveler rather than the general taxpayer. From the standpoint of efficiency, the first result is desirable unless it can be demonstrated that there are external benefits from reducing delays—

benefits that do not accrue to the air traveler. Only to the extent that such benefits exist, and are not themselves matched by external costs, should the price charged for the services be set below the incremental cost of providing them. The second result of charging a price for the service is desirable unless there are public policy reasons for redistributing income from the general taxpayer to the air traveler.

In brief, an examination of the stated objective—the provision of terminal traffic control facilities to meet demand safely and with minimum delays—raises a crucial question: What should be the policy with respect to the price at which the facilities will be furnished? The analytic study of airport traffic delay problems, in turn, gives at least partial evidence that delays may be quite sensitive to the price charged for services, and that delays are primarily a peak load problem which is susceptible to standard, peak-load pricing solutions. In this complex area, systematic analysis is necessary for a meaningful discussion of objectives. And, in turn, a careful consideration of objectives is a prerequisite to intelligent choice among program alternatives.

Let me pursue this illustration several steps further. The analytic study points out that procedural changes in handling aircraft arrivals and departures greatly reduce average delays. Several possibilities exist, including (1) changes in priority procedures for arrivals relative to departures, using criteria relating to aircraft speed classes; (2) segregation of aircraft using various runways according to performance characteristics of the aircraft; and (3) limiting aircraft at airports according to performance characteristics. In other words, the objective for the traffic control program at airports should include not only the provision of *facilities* but also the development and improvement of *procedures* and *regulations*. I do not mean to suggest that FAA gives no thought to procedures, nor that the suggested procedural steps are free from problems. But excessive concentration on the provision of facilities as an objective can lead to unnecessarily expensive solutions to traffic delays.

The different treatment accorded to commercial and general aviation brings out another aspect of the problem of setting objectives. Commercial aviation now pays, through various user charges, a significant proportion of the cost of federal air traffic control facilities (though still less than long-run incremental costs). General aviation pays for only a small fraction of the costs attributable to its use of the airways. General aviation, because of its spectacular growth in recent years, has had a major impact on traffic congestion and delays. During congested periods at airports where general aviation operates from the same runways as commercial carriers, each small aircraft using a runway can increase delay by one minute for every other aircraft using that runway. During a two-hour period of congestion involving 100 commercial aircraft, the total additional delay due to only 10 general aviation flights spread evenly over the two hours would be 500 aircraft-minutes. Assuming a conservative sixty passengers per commercial aircraft flight, these 10 general aviation flights—serving perhaps twenty or thirty passengers— would result in an aggregate delay of 30,000 passenger-minutes or 500 passenger-hours, and additional direct operating costs to the commercial air carriers involved of about $5,000. This is a cost per general aviation flight of $500 and fifty hours of passenger time.

The FAA study of airport delay discusses the effect on delays from the interaction of aircraft using neighboring airports in the same area. In particular, it indicates that projected rapid growth in instrument flight rules (IFR) operations by general aviation, at airports in the vicinity of major air traffic centers will substantially increase commercial aviation delays. Because facilities are made available to meet the growth of noncommercial demand at near zero price for the services rendered, the rate of growth has been stimulated. The consequence is sharp feedback on costs and on time lost by commercial passengers through systems interaction at air terminals. Again, analysis of the system raises substantial questions with respect to program objectives.

This discussion has, necessarily, touched only the surface of an extremely complex problem. But it is a good illustration of the interaction between a careful analysis of system characteristics and the formulation of meaningful program objectives. [Precisely because means and ends are so intertwined, as Lindblom suggests, sophisticated analysis of objectives is a critical component of the decision process. General values with respect to, let us say, the promotion of aviation and to air safety cannot conceivably be translated into meaningful judgments about particular programs without a careful examination of specific program objectives. Nor can effective program alternatives be designed for policy debate without such an examination.] For example, even those who would argue for the maximum possible expansion of aviation should take into account the impact of general aviation operations on congestion, delays, and the consequent deterrent to the growth of air travel.

The HEW study of infant mortality cited earlier provides another example of how analysis is necessary to translate general values into specific objectives. "Do something about the excessive infant mortality rates and chronic handicapping conditions among children in the United States" is not an operationally meaningful goal. It only became possible to reduce this general objective to specifics through analysis of the highly concentrated incidences of infant mortality and handicapping, and an identification of the particular conditions involved in "health-depressed" areas. In the HEW study, several ranges of improvements were analyzed. Alternative programs within each range were designed, their outputs and costs compared, and important constraints examined. The analysis did not recommend a particular program. Rather it described alternative program characteristics so that the relationship between specific outputs and the general objective of improving infant mortality and handicapping conditions could be intelligently examined.

[Analysis of objectives is not only important for program design. It is also needed for program evaluation. Program performance is meaningful only in terms of program objectives] For example, measured solely in terms of subsequent employment and income, vocational rehabilitation programs that principally serve the physically disabled have high benefit-cost ratios, on the order of 10 or 12 to 1. Other programs primarily designed to train the hard-core disadvantaged in central cities tend to have much lower benefit-cost ratios.

This does not imply that one program is necessarily better than the other. From the *partial* benefit-cost studies cited above, the conclusion cannot be drawn that within a limited budget resources should be transferred from the low benefit-cost program to the high one. Both programs aim to raise the productivity and the employment probability of trainees, and in this sense their objectives are the same. But programs to train the hard-core unemployed have additional benefits in terms of an improved social structure which cannot be measured simply in terms of added employment and income. Moreover, the difficulties of achieving a given change in employability and productivity are much less in the vocational rehabilitation program than in the other programs. From an employability standpoint, it is often easier to overcome physical handicaps than social and cultural ones. Evaluation of the two programs will be misleading unless the differences in objectives and in target populations are kept in mind.

Similarly, the Forest Service of the Department of Agriculture has as one of its objectives the provision of recreation opportunities in the national forests. Partial measurements of program output can be constructed in terms of visitor-days capacity, differentiated by various types of recreation facilities. But further analysis of forest service recreation facilities in terms of their location relative to population centers suggests that facilities may be currently out of balance with respect to population. Since proximity to population centers is part of the objectives of a public recreation program, measures of program performance in terms of visitor-days capacity should be distinguished by geographical region and weighted—either quantitatively or judgmentally—by proximity to population.

Both of these examples serve to illustrate the role of the analyst in the translation of broad policy goals into specific program objectives. The determination that public policy should place great weight on job training for the hard-core disadvantaged does not automatically flow from a systematic analysis of national manpower problems—although analysis of costs and the full range of benefits can make an important contribution. The decision is fundamentally a political determination. But the analyst can play a major role in translating that general policy into specific objectives, taking into account job markets and the composition of the target population, and designing program performance measurements in the light of objectives. In the case of the geographical distribution of recreation facilities, program analysis can call the attention of policy makers to the relationship between the location of facility investment and recreation benefits. The systems analyst cannot offer an optimum location policy based on nonpolitical criteria, since major political values are involved in all location decisions, but he can formulate specific alternative objectives for facility investment location. Moreover, given some decision among alternatives by policy makers, he can design measures of program performance suited to the particular objectives. In the recreation facilities case, tactical considerations may dictate that explicit debate about location objectives be muted. Congress might tacitly accept a gradual shift in the proportion of recreational investment made in various regions yet balk at putting its approval on an explicit state.ment of priorities. But considerations of how one publicizes or debates a particular set of policy recommendations should not determine the kind or quality of analysis that underlies the formulation of those recommendations.

[So far, we have been considering the role of systematic analysis as a means of improving the advocacy process. We can agree with Lindblom that the purpose of the advocacy process and political bargaining is to reach decisions about specific programs in the context of conflicting and vaguely known values. Systematic analysis makes a major, and essential, contribution to this process by forging links between general values and specific program characteristics—links that are immediately and directly evident only in the simplest cases. It forges these links, first, by determining social production functions that relate program inputs to program outputs, and, second, by translating general values into operationally specific objectives against which the outputs can be evaluated. Analysis of both objectives and production functions must be a simultaneous process in which better understanding of production functions clarifies objectives, and a clearer knowledge of objectives stimulates the development of alternative production functions.]

[We can also agree with Lindblom that in dealing with the

great uncertainties surrounding complex issues of social policy, sequential decision making is usually a desirable means of making progress. But here too analysis has a major role to play, through systematic program evaluation. Proceeding by trial and error is of no use unless we design the trials meaningfully, recognize the errors promptly, and make the necessary corrections. Where complex issues are involved, we must rely on analysis to help. Intuition and goodwill alone will not suffice.

It is not really important that the analysis be fully accepted by all the participants in the bargaining process. We can hardly expect that information systems will be so complete, necessary assumptions so obviously true, or constraints so universally accepted that a good analysis can be equated with a generally accepted one. But analysis can help focus debate upon matters about which there are real differences of value, where political judgments are necessary. It can suggest superior alternatives, eliminating, or at least minimizing, the number of inferior solutions. Thus, by sharpening the debate, systematic analysis can enormously improve it.

The most frustrating aspect of public life is not the inability to convince others of the merits of a cherished project or policy. Rather, it is the endless hours spent on policy discussions in which the irrelevant issues have not been separated from the relevant, in which ascertainable facts and relationships have not been investigated but are the subject of heated debate, in which consideration of alternatives is impossible because only one proposal has been developed, and, above all, discussions in which nobility of aim is presumed to determine effectiveness of program. There are enough real value conflicts, institutional rigidities, and scarcities of information in the way of effective government action. Let us not add a massive additional obstacle by assuming that complex values can be effectively translated into necessarily complex programs by nothing more than spirited debate. It may, indeed, be necessary to guard against the naiveté of the systems analyst who ignores *political* constraints and believes that efficiency alone produces virtue. But it is equally necessary to guard against the naiveté of the decision maker who ignores *resource* constraints and believes that virtue alone produces efficiency.

5 PPB in a Political Context

One way of defining PPB is simply as a system for bringing analysis to bear on program decisions. Analytic efforts that stay outside of the stream of decisions remain just that—analytic efforts, not instruments for shaping decisions. The crucial element of PPB is that it operates through the budget process. It seeks to bring analysis to bear on decisions by merging analysis, planning, and budgetary allocation. It is a decision structure, and therefore must relate to other elements of the decision process. The purpose of this chapter is to examine how PPB, considered as a system, relates to the political process of adversary bargaining and incremental policy making described by Lindblom.

Incrementalism

The theory of decision making that we have been considering emphasizes incrementalism as a key element in the advocacy or bargaining process. PPB, on the other hand, attempts to modify, if not to replace, incremental budgeting with the examination of a wide range of alternative means toward a given end. Are PPB and systematic analysis unrealistic? Are they positively harmful in terms of disrupting a tried and true incrementalist and gradualist system?

While incremental decisions make up by far the largest proportion of government decisions, they do not encompass the universe of decisions. The massive tax cut of 1964 was not an incremental decision, nor was the passage of the Elementary and Secondary Education Act of 1965, the adoption of Medicare, the Interstate Highway Program, the poverty program, the shift of defense policy from massive retaliation to reliance on graduated response, the 1961 decision for a manned lunar landing in this decade, or the administration's current proposals for building 6

77

million low-cost housing units in ten years. Federal expenditures on education and on health have risen at an average rate of almost 30 percent per year for the past four years, almost tripling in less than half a decade. Only if the concept of "incremental" is defined as anything short of a revolution, would these decisions fit the definition. But if, more realistically, we define a nonincremental policy as one that departs sharply from past practice, or one that requires a very large increase (or decrease) in the commitment of resources to a particular area, then there have been a large number of nonincremental decisions in recent years. And if a decision is not incremental, then certainly the range of alternatives scanned by analysis before the decision is made should not be incremental—it should cover a wide range of choices rather than a narrow one.

This is not to say that political constraints are unimportant when a radical proposal is made, or that efficiency and effectiveness criteria are the only ones to be considered by the decision maker. But large commitments have large consequences, and the reduction of uncertainty about those consequences becomes correspondingly important. Moreover, radical proposals require a particularly careful packaging to attract sufficient support for adoption. Successive alternative program formulations usually are forthcoming, as pieces of the overall package are added, subtracted, or modified in the process of putting together a successful coalition, either before the proposal is submitted to the Congress or during congressional consideration. In this case, the range of alternatives is widened in a search not for efficiency or effectiveness, but for a saleable product. The PPB system can play a highly constructive role by helping the policy maker evaluate various program modifications in terms of a tradeoff between political saleability and program effectiveness. Since decisions whether to accept or reject a proposed amendment or modification often have to be made on relatively short notice, the ideal practice would be to have some range of alternatives— in terms of second or third best solutions—analyzed in advance. Prior cooperation between a department's legislative specialists and its program analysts can yield high payoffs in helping to predict and prepare for possible contingencies while legislation is being considered in the Congress. Analysts who do not like the business of devising second or third or even fourth best alternatives would probably do well to choose other careers.

While in recent years we have witnessed many decisions that were not incremental in nature, it is still true that the number of radical decisions that any political leadership can effect at one time is strictly limited. Most of the individual budget decisions made each year are incremental in nature. But the practice of incremental budgeting is still, as I pointed out in an earlier chapter, a pernicious one. By incremental budgeting I mean the system whereby budget reviews examine only those items for which increases over the prior year are requested. Unless a new program is proposed, there is no examination of basic program structure or performance. It does not bring up alternatives. It does not lend itself to the periodic examination of the objectives of older programs.

In practice, of course, budget reviews have never been purely incremental. Agency heads and their budget officers and the Bureau of the Budget have raised basic questions of program objectives and performance in the context of budgetary decisions. Nevertheless, the whole process was not structured to integrate these kinds of questions into the budget review. In the jargon of the trade, the system did not encourage "zero-base reviews." The base for most reviews was last year's budget level.

PPB is, in theory, zero-base oriented. It does not accept last year's budget as the starting point for analysis, examining only proposed increases or decreases. It seeks to evaluate existing programs in the light of carefully specified program objectives and searches for more effective program alternatives. The program memorandum was designed to evaluate program performance and to propose major budgetary decisions based on that evaluation. This does not imply that every aspect of every program should be reviewed from the ground up each year. A basic program analysis, once completed, does not have to be repeated every budget cycle. PPB's orientation toward zero-base reviews does not mean that we must reevaluate the entire federal program structure every time a budget is put together. Selectivity in the issues raised, in the programs reviewed, and in the range of alternatives examined is crucial to the success of PPB.

No one, of course, ever conceived that PPB would subject every program element to an annual zero-base review. But I must admit that in first establishing PPB procedures in civilian agencies, too little consideration was given to the problem of selectivity.[1] Although agencies were asked to focus on "central questions," the original Budget Bureau instructions could have been interpreted as requiring a comprehensive analysis of all program elements. As a consequence, initial submission of program memoranda from many agencies took up six-foot bookshelves, described (not analyzed) program objectives and content in excruciating detail, and burdened harassed budget examiners with a flood of irrelevant material. Similarly, in the first year of PPB, the Bureau of the Budget requested too many special analytic studies of individual issues. Predictably, given the scarcity of analytical resources, the average quality of the studies suffered sharply, and the submission dates were often so late as to

1. See U.S. Bureau of the Budget, Bulletin No. 66–3 (processed; October 12, 1965), and Supplement to Bulletin No. 66–3 (processed; February 21, 1966).

prohibit meaningful use of even the good studies in the budget process.

Matters have gradually but substantially improved. This year (1968) the Bureau of the Budget has identified, jointly with each agency, a selected number of major issues for consideration in the 1970 budget process. Program memoranda will concentrate upon these issues. This identification singles out particular programs or, more usually, particular aspects of programs for a zero-base review. This approach obviously depends on predicting those issues which will be most important in the 1970 budget review. And like all predictions it will undoubtedly be less than perfect. But this is largely offset by the large gains of selectivity. The 1970 program memoranda will concentrate on a set of major preidentified issues. They will form the principal basis for the 1970 budget review.

In a similar vein, the number of subjects chosen for special in-depth analytic study has been reduced. Studies have been divided into two categories: The first will examine a subset of the issues identified for coverage in the 1970 program memoranda; the second will involve longer-term studies whose submission dates extend beyond the 1970 budget review period, and will lay the groundwork for zero-base program reviews in later years.

As it is evolving, therefore, PPB falls somewhere between purely incremental budgeting and an annual zero-base review of all programs. Incremental budgeting alone—especially when confined to a single budget year rather than a multiyear plan—tends to deny the President, his immediate staff, and his cabinet officers the opportunity to review a significant range of alternatives. It confirms the inertia of existing program arrangements and budgetary allocations and strengthens the power of subordinate bureaus and offices. At the other extreme, an attempt to carry out annual zero-base reviews of all programs has several

81

drawbacks: the political opportunity costs of seeking too many fundamental changes at any one time, the scarcity of analysts capable of providing the necessary background studies, and the limitation on top-level decision-making resources. These considerations limit the number of difficult problems that can be handled in a given time period. PPB is groping for a middle ground between these two extremes.

The Choice of Issues To Analyze

One of the major ingredients of success in this effort will be a perceptive selection of issues to be examined and alternatives to be considered. On the one hand, the PPB system and the program analyst must always be trying to stretch the frontiers of the politically possible. The tension between the analyst's criteria of efficiency and political reality is a healthy one. If PPB, as a system, encourages the analyst always to stay within the boundaries of conventional political wisdom we will make little progress in improving budget review. Yet if PPB goes too far in the other direction, completely ignoring political constraints in the interest of effectiveness and efficiency, overwhelming the decision maker with difficult political choices, and presenting him time after time with alternatives that are far beyond the range of political viability, it will soon discredit itself as a useful tool for decision making. To be successful, PPB must remain a living part of the decision process. It can only do so if it helps the policy maker in terms of specific decisions.

The selection of appropriate issues for examination and the choice of boundaries within which to design realistic alternatives is itself an art. It cannot be governed by a set of formal rules. Yet some general propositions can be laid down, and these may prove useful in the selection of issues and alternatives and, more generally, in defining the role of problem-solving analysis in the political process. These propositions flow from a consideration of the characteristics of governmental programs.

Characteristics of Governmental Programs
as They Affect PPB

There are several ways to categorize government programs. One approach is to place each program's fundamental purpose into one of the three classes defined by recent welfare theory.

1. Production of a *pure public good*—a good which, once provided, is available to all; individuals or groups cannot be excluded from its enjoyment regardless of whether they have contributed to its provision. Consequently, the market system of selling for a price cannot be used as a mechanism to make production and consumption decisions. National defense, law enforcement, and the space program are examples.

2. Production of a *quasi-public good*—a good that could be produced under the private market system, but which carries with it important external benefits or costs. The market system would not produce the good in the appropriate quantity or quality, thus public programs to expand or retard its production or to change its quality are undertaken. Public education, neighborhood health centers, manpower training programs, and many public works projects are examples.

3. A change in the *distribution of income* from what it would be under the market system. The change may relate to distribution among people of different income levels—providing public assistance payments to the poor; it may relate to distribution among people in different occupational groups irrespective of income—farm subsidy programs, for example; it may relate to particular geographical areas—reclamation projects in the West. Governmental programs that change income distribution need not all be designed in terms of shifting income from rich to poor.

83

Many individual programs are a mixture of the last two categories—production of quasi-public goods and redistribution of income. Most federal aid to education, manpower training programs, public health clinics, and irrigation projects have this dual nature. In many cases—such as federal maritime subsidies—the program is publicly justified as a quasi-public good (preserving an American merchant marine for defense purposes), while its major consequences are income redistribution.

In one sense, any program decision affects income distribution. The purchase of fighter aircraft will result in a different distribution of income by income size group and by geographical area than a decision to produce M–16 rifles because the skill composition of the work force and the location of plants is not the same in the two industries. However, some program decisions have a direct and fundamental effect on income distribution. The allocation of public works funds to hydropower rather than to local flood protection has an *incidental* income distribution effect because hydropower includes a large component of hard goods manufacturing in the form of generators and turbines. Flood protection is almost solely construction, and wage scales in the two cases are different. But a decision between them would also have a *fundamental* income distribution effect because those who receive electricity from federal hydropower projects pay for most of the costs, while beneficiaries of flood protection do not. It is the fundamental and direct, rather than the incidental, income distribution effect that is relevant for the classification discussed here.

Another classification of governmental programs may be based on whether choices of detailed program specifications or of specific program objectives significantly affect the structure and relationships of political and institutional power. Whether assistance under Title III of the Elementary and Secondary

Education Act remains in the form of federal project grants or is parceled out on a formula basis through state boards of education has an impact on the locus of educational decision-making power. "Participation of the poor" in the governing bodies of the poverty program's Community Action agencies is a dramatic illustration of the struggle for political power. The form and content of federal manpower training programs affect the influence of local labor unions on the kind of training provided by the programs, which in turn has an important impact on the local labor market. The extent to which low-income-housing subsidy programs should be subject to local planning requirements has a major effect on the survival of various protective devices through which local institutions have discriminated in the supply of housing according to income and race. Federal programs vary widely according to whether choices about their detailed provisions impinge on the structure and distribution of power.

These two classifications are by no means completely independent of each other. Detailed decisions about programs that mix income distribution and quasi-public-good objectives—like the provision of neighborhood health clinics or aid to education—are more likely to raise questions of political power structures than are detailed decisions on how to produce a pure public good, such as the decision on the specific mix of manned and unmanned flights in the space program. Where a program fits in one set of classifications helps to determine where it fits in the others. The constraints on problem-solving analysis in applying efficiency and effectiveness criteria and the range of alternatives that it is worthwhile to consider vary substantially according to where a particular program falls in the classifications suggested above.

I propose as a working hypothesis that analysis can operate

with fewer constraints and can profit from consideration of a wider range of alternatives in programs that produce a pure public good and do not directly affect the structure of institutional and political power than in programs that produce a quasi-public good, fundamentally affect income distribution, or impinge on the power structure. Among the major programs falling in the former classification are defense, space, the Atomic Energy Commission's weapons production and testing, and overseas information programs. With certain important qualifications, the Post Office could be put in this category, even though it represents a largely private good produced by a public body.

Let me be quite clear about my meaning. Basic choices about national policy and the overall magnitude of resources devoted to them are no less political and value oriented in the case of pure public goods than in any other programs. In fact, fundamental program choices with respect to such goods have important connotations for the structure of power in society— witness the perennial discussion of the influence of the military-industrial complex. Concern over the effects of incidental income distribution—what plants, industries, or locations are chosen for producing public goods—arouse strong political pressures. But in the case of pure public goods, once broad program decisions are made, the specification of detailed objectives and the choice of detailed means of production have less impact on income redistribution and on the locus of power than do detailed discussions in other governmental programs.

The basic reason that detailed decisions concerning the nature and means of producing public goods have less political content than equally detailed decisions on other government programs is that such decisions are primarily technical in nature. The specific characteristics of a nuclear research reactor, a space capsule, or the mix of airlift and sealift raise quite different kinds of questions than do the detailed provisions of an aid-to-education bill, a poverty program, or a farm price subsidy. In other words, once the decision to produce a purely public good has been made, the production function chosen for that good (or for a private good produced by a public body) is less likely to have an impact on income distribution or political power than in other types of programs.[2]

In most federal programs directly affecting income distribution, or producing a quasi-public good, choices involving basic political values permeate every level of decision making. The specification and tradeoff among objectives and the selection of particular production functions almost inevitably have a direct impact on intensely held values. To the extent that the analyst is seeking to maximize effectiveness, given a broad statement of goals and a particular budget allocation, or efficiency, given a specified set of objectives, he is likely to face many more outside constraints in these programs than in the case of pure-public-goods programs.

The fact that most of the social programs of the federal government fall in the categories that tend to place additional constraints on the use of systematic analysis in no sense detracts from the importance of analysis. It is precisely because analysis is underdeveloped in these areas, and because the knowledge of production functions is so difficult to acquire and yet so critical, that substantially more resources need to be devoted to analysis. My argument here is that the selection of issues worth examining and the range of alternatives it is profitable to pursue need to be chosen with full knowledge of political constraints. This is a job for both the decision makers who determine analytical as-

2. Expressed another way, in public goods programs it is possible to suboptimize at a higher level of objectives than in other governmental programs, where numerous political constraints enter at a very low level of optimization.

signments and the analysts who, while trying to extend the frontiers of the possible, must at the same time develop political sensitivities—not so much to avoid delicate issues as to recognize them.

There is, I think, still another set of distinctions that can be made about governmental programs, which has relevance for the selection of issues to be analyzed and alternatives to be considered. While still faced with a formidable array of political constraints, analysis based on efficiency and effectiveness criteria has a much greater chance to affect the shape and direction of new and rapidly expanding programs than it does to reform existing programs which have a heavy component of income redistribution. There are, undoubtedly, fewer constraints on how new benefits are distributed than on removing long-existing ones. Although most of the new social programs do involve some income redistribution, the connection between the new program and the loss of income through higher taxes or smaller program benefits elsewhere is hard to trace. Each "loser" pays only a small fraction of his income to any particular program. But reform of older subsidy programs—farm, irrigation, maritime, or veterans—threatens a relatively homogeneous and well-organized group with a direct and substantial loss of income. Building efficiency and effectiveness into new programs may affect potential beneficiaries with a loss of potential benefits. But human nature being what it is, this is far less difficult to do than taking actual benefits away from actual beneficiaries.

It is somewhat paradoxical that in precisely those programs such as agriculture, public works, maritime subsidies, and the like, where there are relatively good data, where market prices can provide at least an initial guide to the evaluation of output, and where a long tradition of theoretical and empirical work exists that program analysis is faced with the greatest political constraints. On the other hand, in those growing social programs whose very newness offers a wider range of political options, analysis is faced with severe constraints by the scarcity of data and by a rudimentary theoretical background. What we can do best analytically we find hardest to achieve politically. Where we have a greater freedom from political constraint we have the least analytical preparation. This may illustrate some fundamental law of human affairs, but if so I have not yet been able to discover it.

If the hypothesis I have stated above is correct, the range of alternatives which it is practically worthwhile for the systems analyst to scan is significantly broader in the design of the new and burgeoning social programs of government than for those of existing subsidy programs. This does not mean that attempts at program reform should be abandoned, but that the economy of political resources sharply limits the number of basic reforms that can realistically be pursued at any one time. In the case of established programs that benefit particular groups in society, the most useful analysis to the policy maker is often one that scans a relatively narrow range of alternatives looking toward incremental improvements.

The fact that in the older subsidy programs most improvements will probably have to be incremental does not mean that analysts outside the government—in universities and research institutions—should abandon research aimed at more radical reform. Rather, increased public knowledge of the inefficiencies and perverse income distribution effects of some federal programs helps widen the range of feasible alternatives facing the systems analyst in government.

In the case of farm commodity supports, for example, recent studies of farm income distribution have shown that in 1966 the 16 percent of farms with sales of $20,000 and over accounted for

68 percent of all cash receipts from farming, and taking into account nonfarm income, had an average net income of $19,800.[3] Since the benefits of federal farm programs are roughly proportional to production volume, this means that about two-thirds of federal farm subsidy benefits accrued to the upper one-sixth of the farm population, whose average net income was almost $20,000. Similar concentrations of benefits among upper-income farmers become evident when individual crops are studied.[4] The top 20 percent of wheat farmers, in terms of size of acreage allotment, received 62 percent of price support benefits; the top 20 percent of cotton farmers, 69 percent of benefits; the top 20 percent of sugar cane growers, 83 percent of benefits; and so on. In any case, the farm commodity support program is not an income maintenance program primarily aimed at low-income groups.

Even more striking results occur in the irrigation projects of the Bureau of Reclamation. Analysis of a representative cross-section of irrigation projects started since 1964, covering projects with an aggregate capital cost allocated to irrigation of $574 million, shows that the cost per farm *averaged* $132,000. The average present value of repayments required from irrigators, calculated at a 5 percent discount rate and a fifty-year life, was only $10,000. The average subsidy *per farm*, therefore, was $122,000. Looked at another way, the subsidy per farm is equivalent to the present value of a $6,700 annual payment made every year for fifty years. Part of the subsidy is paid by the federal government, the remainder by consumers of hydro-

3. U.S. Department of Agriculture, *Farm Income Situation* (July 1967), pp. 68–73.

4. These studies were carried out by James T. Bonnen, "The Distribution of Benefits from Selected U.S. Farm Programs" (processed; paper prepared for the U.S. National Advisory Commission on Rural Poverty, 1967).

electric power whose rates are set to cover some of the irrigation subsidy.

More dramatic examples of income distribution consequences can be found. In many parts of Southern California, irrigators pay $2.80 per acre-foot for water from federal projects. The value of water for other uses is about $35 per acre-foot.[5] A typical 320-acre cotton farm will use about 1,300 acre-feet per year. The opportunity cost of the subsidy to such a farm is, therefore, about $42,000 *per year*. The same farm may grow 450 bales of cotton per year, receiving an average subsidy of $28,000 on its cotton production. The two subsidies combined are worth $70,000 per year. The subsidy cost of placing one low-income family in decent housing averages about $800 per year. In terms of tradeoffs, therefore, the continuation of irrigation and commodity subsidies implies that public policy considers the maintenance of this particular farm in irrigated cotton production to be worth the placing of 90 low-income families in decent housing. Often the combined value of irrigation and commodity subsidies is substantially greater than the net income of the recipient, since part of the subsidy must go simply to bringing him up to a break-even point. (After all, it is hard to cover the full economic costs of growing watermelons in the desert, but it is relatively profitable for the grower when water is provided at $2.80 per acre-foot.) It would be cheaper to buy out many irrigated farm operators with an annuity contract paying an annual amount equal to their full current income.

It may often be unprofitable for the in-house governmental analyst to scan the full range of alternatives because of severe

5. This assumes a $70 per acre-foot value of water delivered to Los Angeles, less a $35 per acre-foot cost for delivery of water from the Colorado River to Los Angeles. See Jack Hirshleifer, James C. DeHaven, and Jerome W Milliman, *Water Supply: Economics, Technology, and Policy* (University of Chicago Press, 1960), pp. 318–35.

limitations imposed by political constraints. But the key point is that those constraints are not immutable. They are affected by changes in public attitudes. In the case of well-established, producer-group subsidy programs, the criteria for selection of issues to be given a zero-base review and the range of alternatives to be considered may indeed be quite confining, if the PPB system is to avoid breaking its limited supply of analytical lances against windmills. But the *outside* analyst can perform a highly effective role across a much wider range of options. The fruits of his analysis can help remove some of the constraints faced by the governmental analyst.

We have examined the role of systematic analysis in the governmental decision process and found it to be a complement to and in tension with political dialogue. Systematic analysis complements the advocacy process by articulating the links between general values on the one hand and specific program characteristics on the other. It is in tension with political dialogue because it emphasizes resource efficiency and stresses economic opportunity costs, while political dialogue has its own set of efficiency criteria and emphasizes political opportunity costs. The effective use of systematic analysis, therefore, requires a recognition of political constraints and political opportunity costs in the selection of issues and the choice of alternatives to be examined. Developing a sense of what constraints to recognize and of when and how far to stretch those constraints is an essential attribute of a good analytic team.

PPB and the Power Structure

I have indicated that PPB can be a means of strengthening the role of department heads in their relations with subordinate operating units. There are three ways in which this occurs.

First, to the extent that the agency head uses output-oriented program categories for making broad, strategic, budget decisions, he cuts across organizational lines. (Output boundaries rarely match organizational boundaries.) In turn, subordinate bureaus are forced to justify proposed program expansions in terms of output. And given normal bureaucratic inertia, decisions about changes in the composition of output are more likely to be initiated at the secretarial level than in operating bureaus.

Second, by drawing up a tentative program and financial plan as a starting point for budget submissions, agency heads can more likely influence the broad allocation of resources within a department. The preparation of the 1969 budget in HEW is an example. A list of significant issues was developed early in the year and discussed within the department and with the Bureau of the Budget. Next, the secretary asked each operating agency to formulate tentative objectives for 1973, in program categories and in terms of both budget dollars and program content. Two alternative 1973 budgetary ceilings—a "high" and a "low"—were assigned each operating agency. The submissions were reviewed by the secretary who then formulated a set of departmental objectives for 1973, reflecting his own evaluation of priorities. The results of his review were delivered to the operating agencies, together with an initial 1969 budget ceiling, to serve as the basis for detailed budget submission for the forthcoming fiscal year. Under this system, budget submissions for the coming year did not just "bubble up" to the secretary in response to a "call for estimates"; nor were they derived from program decisions unilaterally imposed by the secretary. They were developed in a joint dialogue between the secretary, his immediate staff, and the operating agency heads in an attempt to formulate the next year's budget in the context of long-range strategy for the department.

Third, program planning and evaluation staffs in the agency head's immediate office, created by the PPB system, strengthen the role of the agency head in relations with the operating units. Cynics to the contrary notwithstanding, knowledge is power. An agency head's ability to control the direction his department takes depends in part on his being able to face his operating subordinates with information and analysis about their own programs. In one sense, he must know as much about the important aspects of their operations as they do. Operating administrators are often far more able to call up political resources in the form of constituent groups or congressional subcommittees than is an agency head. In some cases, information and analysis is the only weapon a secretary has. An analytically capable PPB staff can be a major source of strength for an agency head, if he is willing to use it. It is precisely for this reason that some—though by no means all—members of Congress have been, to say the least, less than enthusiastic about the development of PPB. Very often strengthening the position of the secretary means reducing the power of the congressional committees and subcommittees which have direct lines of communication with and influence over individual operating units.

The redistribution of power from subordinate units to agency heads could, of course, go too far. There is no law of nature that allocates to cabinet secretaries the wisdom and objectivity of a Solomon and to subordinate bureaucracies a callous unconcern for the broader aspects of the public interest. At the moment, however, I think the balance of power lies too much against most agency heads. All of us, quite properly, play roles that are, in part, dictated by our positions. And the secretary of a department is more likely to be able to balance conflicting values and to scan a wider range of alternatives than is any single operating unit. I do not believe that in the typical executive department the power of the secretary is commensurate with his responsibility. PPB can, and in some cases has, I think, helped modestly to redress the balance.

I might add, as an aside, that the situation in the typical state and municipal government is even more unbalanced. Partly due to a lack of central staff, many governors, and I venture most mayors, find it exceedingly difficult to control their own operating departments. The current efforts to introduce PPB into state and local governments could have a high payoff, if for no other reason than that they offer a means of providing the chief executive with a modicum of central staff resources.

There is still another role for PPB to play in the political process. Decision making is done by advocacy and bargaining. PPB introduces the "efficiency partisan" into the debate. At the bureau level, the program evaluation staff, to be effective, must operate within the constraints and basic values associated with that bureau. They are, however, more likely to be interested in questions of efficiency than the rest of the bureau. Given the current values and constraints of the bureau, the program evaluation staff can be expected to promote the selection of efficient means of achieving the bureau's values. The total level of resources going to the bureau may, indeed, be too large, viewed from some outside vantage point. And part of the program analyst's time may well be devoted to helping his bureau chief protect those excessive resources. Nevertheless, given a budget level however determined, the program evaluation staff can be advocates for optimizing the use of that budget from the standpoint of effectiveness and efficiency. They can also be advocates for testing, at the margin, the elasticity of those constraints that reduce the efficiency with which the bureau's resources are used.

At the departmental level, analytic staffs will be bound by the values and constraints of the department. They, too, can be ex-

pected to pay more attention to efficiency and effectiveness criteria than other staffs in the department. They can scan a wider
range of alternatives and tradeoffs than their counterparts in
operating bureaus. From an outside viewpoint, they too may be
suboptimizing,[6] but at a more comprehensive level.

Analysts at the Bureau of the Budget can and should play the
role of efficiency advocates at a still higher level. In short, the
PPB system provides the decision process with a new group of
advocates. They are, in effect, "partisan efficiency advocates"—
the champions of analysis and efficiency. They are indeed par-
tisans, and the ultimate decision maker has to balance their
voice against political, tactical, and other considerations. The
number of constraints within which these advocates seek to
optimize increases as we proceed down the decision-making
scale, from Executive Office of the President, through departmental staffs, to operating bureau staffs. If we seek the same
level of optimization from each level, we will necessarily be
frustrated. But if we recognize that the constraints are a function
of the level of decision making, and that the analytic staffs are
themselves advocates in the decision process—not final decision

6. The concept of suboptimizing relates to the problem of achieving efficiency
when faced with a number of constraints. For example, if asked to design a federal investment program to increase income in the lower Colorado basin, using a
specified amount of funds, an analyst might propose a series of public facility
investments to attract industry into the area. If political considerations require
that the funds be used only for water resource projects, he would perhaps design a
project to increase municipal and industrial water supply. Because his alternatives
have been limited to water supply projects, the resulting program may be less
effective in raising income than other forms of investment, but the analyst would
still seek the optimum design of a water resources project. Should political consideration require an even narrower constraint, for example that the project provide
only irrigation water, the analyst would have to suboptimize at a lower level, his
alternatives having been narrowed still further. But he would seek the optimum
design of an irrigation project.

makers—planning and programming can be effectively integrated with budgeting.

Multiyear Planning

In an earlier chapter I spoke about multiyear planning. There are two quite different approaches to this problem, and choosing between them poses a real dilemma.

On the one hand, the multiyear plan could include only future consequences of currently proposed decisions. Under this method, the five-year plan accompanying the budget submission would propose decisions for the first year and show, for the subsequent four years, both the output and financial costs of proposed and prior decisions. The Bureau of the Budget's instructions to agencies for preparing a program and financial plan for the 1970 budget submission call for this approach, as they did last year. The instructions also provide that when final budget decisions are made, the forward year projections will be modified to conform to those decisions.

Information furnished by the program and financial plan can be combined with estimates of expected workload increases in service agencies such as the Internal Revenue Service, the Federal Aviation Administration, and the Immigration and Naturalization Service. Together these estimates provide, by program, by agency, and for the government as a whole, a means of predicting the built-in increases that the subsequent budget will face.

Over the past five years, federal budget outlays on domestic programs have risen sharply. Under these circumstances, one would expect that decision makers would have had substantial flexibility in directing the course of spending according to their perceptions of priorities. In practice, however, the built-in increases every year, stemming from prior year decisions, have absorbed a large fraction of each single year's budget increase. The size of these built-in increases has always come as a surprise. Available options in any single year have consequently been much smaller than one would surmise simply by looking at the size of the aggregate five-year increase. An information system that provides an aggregate measure of built-in increases, and tags each major decision with its future year consequences in the context of that aggregate, at least indicates to decision makers what their current decisions are doing to their future options. I am firmly convinced that this offers hope for major improvement in the decision process.

While this approach to multiyear planning has many advantages, it also has weaknesses. It does not set multiyear objectives, insofar as reaching those objectives requires budgetary decisions beyond the coming fiscal year. But many programs require that current year decisions be made in the context of longer-term targets. A program started this year may make sense only if there is a reasonable chance of expanding it in subsequent years. When Head Start Follow Through is up for consideration as an operating rather than an experimental program, it may deserve high priority as a potential program only if it can be expanded to cover a substantial number of poor children. A firm decision on how fast the program should be expanded to such a level need not be made initially. But it is conceivable that other programs would take higher priority if Head Start Follow Through ended up covering only one-fifth of eligible poor children. The model cities program is another example. Its success will depend on, among other things, achieving a critical mass in selected urban neighborhoods. Given the easily predictable fact that Congress will require the extension of the program to a large number of cities, funding of the model cities program will have to reach a certain minimum size if it is to be effective. While decisions concerning the specific rate at which the program grows, or its magnitude beyond the minimum effective level, do not need to be made initially and can be adjusted to overall budgetary constraints and pressures from other priorities, the decision to undertake the program in the first place should be made in the context of longer-range objectives and priorities. Does a model cities program of the minimum effective size have higher priority than the items it must necessarily displace?

In these cases we are not dealing with known future consequences of current decisions in the sense that today's decision technically, legally, or morally commits tomorrow's budgetary resources. They are not built-in increases. Rather, we are dealing with what I can only describe as efficiency and effectiveness commitments. Certain programs launched today take priority in the use of budgetary resources over other programs only if, at some future time, they can reach a certain minimum level. If, at that level, they would absorb too large a proportion of available budget resources, relative to other priority needs, then a different pattern of resource allocations should be considered which may exclude these programs altogether.

Agency heads will be in a better position to make current decisions if they have some tentative plans about long-run strategy and resource allocation. For this purpose multiyear plans that incorporate rough projections of decisions not proposed for immediate resolution are required. The development of such plans, however, poses special problems. Unless executive agencies are given some overall budgetary constraints, their longer-range projections tend to be excessively optimistic in terms of the resources that are likely to be available. They are often "pie-in-the-sky" estimates. Consequently, they may be useless for meaningful planning. Some constraints are necessary. But who decides the level and distribution of the longer-term constraints? Further, what is the status of these projections? They incorporate decisions not yet made or not even proposed for resolution in the current budget cycle. No planning mechanism should force a policy maker to decide prematurely. If, as is sure to happen, circumstances force a change in the planned allocations, will operating units be resistant to necessary program modifications because of built-up expectations?

There is no easy way out of this dilemma. But I think a reasonable middle ground might be as follows: First, the detailed program and financial plan should continue to carry only the future consequences of current and prior decisions. Second, the Bureau of the Budget should furnish each agency with two alternative planning constraints expressed in budgetary totals for the agency for the following five years: a "high" estimate based on the assumption of full employment and no change in tax rates—all of the fiscal dividend is assumed to be taken up by increased expenditures; and a "low" estimate based on the assumption that some significant part of the fiscal dividend would be absorbed either by tax reductions or by revenue sharing with state and local governments. Third, the agency head should develop tentative long-term budget projections based on these constraints. These projections would serve two purposes. They would be a means by which the agency head could organize his own thinking about long-term strategy for the agency. They would also be a means of calling attention to those current decisions, such as the model cities and Head Start programs cited above, that make sense only if substantial additional resources are devoted to them in the future. The commitment implied is not precise enough in either timing or magnitude to be included in the program and financial plan. But it should be taken into account in making current decisions.

For all the obvious reasons, the long-term projections I have described above should be treated as informal and tentative, as means in the process of reaching decisions, not as the end result of the process. In the face of uncertainty and a scarcity of relevant information, every agency must retain the freedom to adapt to changing circumstances and knowledge. But flexibility is not the same as absence of planning. However much Lewis and Clark adapted their route to the terrain, they were, after all, guided by the goal of reaching the Pacific Coast, rather than South America or the North Pole.

Conclusion

If PPB is to survive as a system, it must fit into the political process and at the same time must modify that process. I have offered the view that the effectiveness, and indeed survival, of PPB will depend on recognizing, but not slavishly following, political constraints in the selection of issues to be examined and alternatives to be considered. The severity of those constraints varies substantially from program to program, although not in a completely unpredictable way.

In one sense PPB can be viewed as introducing a new set of participants into the decision process, which for want of a better term, I have labeled partisan efficiency advocates. At each level of the decision process these participants become particular champions of efficiency and effectiveness as criteria in decision making. But the values and constraints that the advocates take as given and the range of tradeoffs they may be expected to consider become narrower the lower down they are in the decision hierarchy. So long as the system recognizes this fact, and does not ask the impossible of the various players, it can be an effective component of the advocacy process.

PPB also tends to modify the political process in another way:

101

it improves the capability of the agency head to shape the program of his agency, and increases his power relative to his operating subordinates. Theoretically, this shift in power could go too far, but at the present I feel that some movement in this direction is needed.

Finally, PPB raises quite difficult problems in the area of long-term planning. I have suggested an approach to this problem which, I hope, avoids some of the major political problems that long-range planning typically encounters.

6 Future Directions for Analysis

These lectures have posed, and hopefully answered, the question "How can systematic analysis be effectively applied to governmental decisions that are reached through the essentially political process of advocacy, bargaining, and negotiated solutions?" But consideration of current political and institutional facts of life are not only relevant in defining and legitimizing the role of analysis, they also suggest several specific directions for the future application of systematic analysis to public policy decisions.

Incentives, Rewards, and Penalties

"Systematic" in the term systematic analysis has more than decorative meaning. It implies that problems should be analyzed in the context of the relevant environment. Successful analysis of the federal government's domestic programs does not isolate facts or relationships from the system in which they exist. It does not ignore the feedbacks between results and initial conditions or major spillovers of costs or benefits. It avoids solutions that have a high risk of failure because they run directly across the grain of the system on which they are imposed.

Yet in designing governmental policies that affect domestic social institutions we often ignore the system of incentives, political processes, and administrative organizations within which the policies must be carried out. In well-controlled "command systems" solutions can, to a degree, be imposed directly from the top. But in programs of education, health, crime control, urban development, pollution abatement, and the like, we must deal with a multiplicity of state and local governments and with a powerful web of private incentives and relationships. A well-designed plan and a fistful of money will not be sufficient to achieve the objectives of federal programs if the

103

plan runs counter to the motivations, rewards, and penalties of the public and private institutions that must carry it out.

More particularly, there is a tendency to concentrate on identifying desirable social outcomes in detail and on providing funds to state, local, and private organizations who develop plans that promise to achieve those objectives. The typical federal social program provides a grant of money conditioned on the preparation, by the recipient, of an "acceptable" plan to accomplish the purpose of the particular program. There are hundreds of different program planning requirements. In terms of what they propose to accomplish, these plans often meet the objectives of the program. But the gap between plan and action, between promise and performance is very wide indeed.

We design "Year 2000" plans for our cities. Then the inevitable zoning changes tear the plan to pieces in response to the powerful economic rewards for land development that go completely counter to the plan. We spend hundreds of millions each year for flood protection works, and still the flood costs mount as economic pressures generate more and more intensive development of lands that have a high risk of flooding. We formulate comprehensive social and physical plans for the rehabilitation of slum neighborhoods, only to watch them be delayed and eroded because there are no institutional means to organize the host of different agencies and institutions involved in executing the plans.

The failure of performance stems from two related causes. The first of these is "negative failure"—the failure to take account of private incentives that run counter to program objectives, and to provide for appropriate modifications in existing rewards and penalties that thwart social objectives. Thus, federal, state, and local programs often run the risk of failure because they ignore powerful incentive systems whose rewards and penalties encourage precisely the opposite results of those sought by the program. Under such circumstances even the best administered programs are likely to be impotent.

The second cause is "positive failure"—the failure to build into federal programs a positive set of incentives to channel the activities of decentralized administrators and program operators toward the program objectives. The federal government has over 400 different programs addressed to domestic social problems. More than half were initiated in the last four years. Unlike many of the traditional federal activities—Post Office, veterans' benefits, farm price supports, security exchange regulations, and the like—these programs are not directly administered by the federal government on a uniform national basis. Rather, they are grant-in-aid programs to state or municipal governments or nonprofit local institutions seeking to change social conditions in thousands of communities and tens of thousands of neighborhoods and school districts. Although they reflect public awareness of problems of national significance, they must cope with situations that vary widely from state to state and community to community. The ability of a central staff in Washington to judge the quality and practicality of the thousands of local plans submitted under federal program requirements and to control their performance is severely limited in terms of knowledge of local conditions, administrative efficiency, and political feasibility.

A growing awareness of these problems coupled with the demand, principally by the urban Negro community, for greater control over programs affecting the local neighborhood, has led to a call for decentralization—decentralization of both policy making and administration. I believe that moves toward greater decentralization in the government's social programs should and will be made. And I am aware that a large part of the attraction of decentralization has little to do with the effectiveness of substantive programs and much to do with the simple desire for local participation in the exercise of power. But let us not go so far as to write off the problem of program substance. Regardless of who makes the decisions, it is still important that urban rehabilitation programs actually rehabilitate neighborhoods, manpower training programs successfully train people, and education programs educate youngsters. It is in this sense that the success of decentralization will hinge, to an important degree, on developing appropriate incentive systems. Devising programs to provide incentives for the effective and efficient pursuit of overall program objectives is an area to which systematic analysis should devote increasing attention. It is a problem particularly suited to systematic analysis because it involves the behavior of an interacting system, the federal government being only one part. But the role of the federal government must be designed to channel the entire system toward the desired objectives. Moreover, the development of incentive systems requires that particular attention be paid to the careful specification of objectives and the measurement of performance in the light of those objectives. We must, after all, first decide what it really is that we wish to provide rewards for or penalties against before we can devise positive incentive schemes or modify existing ones.

The examples that follow show several decentralized incentive systems which have been designed or are being experimented with. I also suggest other areas in which the application of systematic analysis to the incentive problem might produce large payoffs. Not all of these examples relate to the social programs of the federal government. But they all exemplify some of the basic principles involved.

Flood Control

Federal investment in flood protection and prevention through the Corps of Engineers and the Soil Conservation Service has totaled in excess of $7 billion since a national flood control policy was adopted in 1936. The current rate of expenditures on flood protection is about $500 million per year, and is increasing. Other federal programs provide disaster relief assistance to flood victims through various loan and grant programs. In 1968, estimated budget obligations for disaster relief programs exceeded $150 million, with the largest part being attributed to flood-related disasters. While estimates of national flood losses are very approximate, they exceed $1 billion per year, and are also increasing.[1]

Until recently, national policy toward flood losses was quite straightforward—build flood protection and prevention works primarily at public expense and assist states, localities, and individuals in recovering large flood losses. This policy has been counterproductive: it sets up incentives for uneconomic development of flood plains.

Once the flood plain is developed, then the standard benefit-cost calculation will often show that the construction of flood prevention or protection works is worthwhile in terms of expected damage avoided. However, in many cases the preferred alternative would have been less intensive development of the flood plain land or no development at all. In other words, the *differential* advantage of the flood plain over the next best alternative is worth less than either the cost of flood protection works or the expected value of damage. Since states, local communities, and individual beneficiaries typically contribute

1. *A Unified National Program for Managing Flood Losses*, Communication from the President of the United States Transmitting a Report by the Task Force on Federal Flood Control Policy, H. Doc. 465, 89 Cong. 2 sess. (1966), p. 3.

only a fraction of the cost of federal flood protection works (ranging from 5 percent to 60 percent and averaging 25 percent), a set of incentives has developed for uneconomic use of flood plain lands. After some development of flood plains, strong and often successful pressure is applied for federal flood protection, either in response to or in anticipation of floods. This leads to federal construction and then to development beyond the protected areas. The resulting encroachment on the flood plain raises expected flood heights, increases the expected flood damage to prior investments, and leads to still further flood protection works. In many cases, floodproofing of individual buildings would be much cheaper than building public flood-control projects. But the costs of floodproofing are borne by the individual owner; the costs of public works are not. Studies of flood plain use "show that some flood plain encroachment is undertaken in ignorance of the hazard, that some occurs in anticipation of further federal protection, and that some takes place because it is profitable for private owners even though it imposes heavy burdens on society."[2]

In earlier years, most flood control projects were justified on the basis of protecting existing developments. More recently, however, an increasing proportion of flood control projects have been justified on the basis of protecting land for future development. It is the absolute value of the potential development that is taken into account rather than the differential value of the site compared to the next best alternative location. This tends to accelerate still further the "cycle of losses, partial protection, further induced (though submarginal) development, and more unnecessary losses."[3]

In 1965, the administration appointed a Task Force on Federal Flood Control Policy, headed by Professor Gilbert

2. *Ibid.*, p. 11.
3. *Ibid.*, p. 12.

108

White of the University of Chicago. The Task Force's report,[4] submitted in 1966, made a series of recommendations to improve flood control policy. These recommendations were all part of an integrated approach to the problem. The incentive features of the recommendations can be summarized briefly.

Ideally, "an effective approach would alter the price signals received by potential flood plain developers." The full costs of flood plain occupancy would be shifted to prospective occupants through an occupancy charge equal to estimated annual damages plus any external costs which development on the plains causes others, as it raises the height of floods. These payments would, in turn, be used to compensate those suffering flood plain damages. Flood control works with benefit-cost ratios greater than unity would lower the annual occupancy charges by more than the cost of undertaking the project. They would be "profitable" to undertake, and the costs of the project would be assessed to those whose occupancy charges had been lowered.

As initial steps in this direction, the report recommended the careful experimentation with and development of a flood-risk insurance program, with premiums on future investment in flood plain land related to flood damage risk. Ultimately, such insurance would be required for an investor in flood-prone lands to be eligible for federal loans, loan guarantees, flood protection investment, or other similar assistance. The development of such a program must be gradual, since premiums seriously out of line with actuarial risk would invite uneconomic location and heavy costs. As a corollary to this recommendation, the report urged a sharply expanded program for determining flood hazards, flood frequency, and expected flood damage. Without such

4. *Ibid.*

109

information, economically meaningful premiums cannot be developed and, to stress again, an insurance program with a poor premium structure is worse than no program at all.

Should an insurance program be developed, with premiums related to risks, failure to charge beneficiaries the cost of installing flood protection works would continue to generate excessive development in the flood plains. Consequently, the report also recommended the development of a cost-sharing formula for flood control works that would more nearly assign the costs to the beneficiaries. Requiring beneficiaries to pay for the cost of public works would tend to neutralize the present bias against investment in the floodproofing of individual structures. Where flood control projects are justified on grounds of benefits from future development, as opposed to the protection of existing investments, the report urges that only *net* locational benefits be taken into account—that is, only the excess value of flood plain location over the next best alternative should be counted in measuring project benefits.

This gives only a partial review of the Task Force's recommendations. But it brings out the essential thrust of the report: a definition of federal flood policy in terms of an economic use of flood plain lands, and the development of a series of recommendations which establish incentives for individual investors and communities to seek this objective.

Subsequent to the submission of the report, the administration initiated steps to begin carrying out its recommendations, including the development of a flood insurance proposal, assigning to the Federal Water Resources Council responsibility for modifying flood control cost-sharing policies, and budget requests to the Congress for funds to improve flood hazard information.

110

Hospital Costs

During the past several years, hospital costs have been rising at a highly accelerated rate. In 1967, they rose by more than 16 percent for the second year in a row. Average per diem hospital costs now approach $65, and have been projected to rise to $100 within five years.[5] If the rate of increase in hospital costs could be reduced by only 2 percent per year, the resulting savings would amount to $5 billion annually by 1975. Hospital utilization, in terms of hospital-days per thousand population, has also been increasing rapidly. Per capita utilization of hospital services rose by 57 percent over the 1955 to 1965 decade. (Part of this rise reflects an excessive use of hospital services relative to patients' needs.) If a 25 percent reduction in hospital utilization rates could be effected, without reducing the quality of patient care, an annual savings in medical costs of $7.5 billion could be realized by 1975.[6]

The federal government's Medicare and Medicaid programs now pay for the hospital care of a significant part of the population. (Built into these programs is the concept of fully reimbursing hospitals for the costs associated with Medicare and Medicaid patients.) Through these programs the federal government can have a major impact on hospital costs, both directly and through its influence on the practices of Blue Cross and commercial insurance carriers.

The objective of reducing hospital costs can be divided into

5. U.S. Department of Health, Education, and Welfare, Secretary's Advisory Committee on Hospital Effectiveness, "Report" (processed; 1967), p. 10.

6. Per capita data are from *Report of the National Advisory Commission on Health Manpower*, Vol. I (U.S. Government Printing Office, 1967), Appendix I, Tables 2 and 4, pp. 88 and 90. The per capita increase in average daily hospital beds used (17 percent) was combined with the increase in the deflated value of service per patient-day to arrive at the 57 percent figure used in the text. The savings data are from p. 68.

two parts: improving the efficiency with which individual hospitals deliver services, and reducing unnecessary utilization of those services.[7] At the present time, federal reimbursement formulas undoubtedly contribute to inefficiency in internal hospital operations. Each hospital is reimbursed for the "reasonable costs" of delivering services to patients under Medicare and Medicaid programs. Payment is matched to the individual costs of each hospital. There are virtually no incentives for efficiency; any savings from more efficient operations result in lower federal payments; any increased costs are fully passed on. To the extent that larger staffs bring prestige and promotion, there are positive incentives for inefficiency. Moreover, since policies in most hospitals are controlled by the physicians serving it, and since the hospital provides a free workshop for those physicians, there are powerful incentives to upgrade the workshop, especially when the costs for most patients are reimbursed by government programs or private insurance carriers.

All the evidence indicates that there is substantial room for improving efficiency in hospital services. For example, 1965 data show that average per diem costs in voluntary, short-term teaching hospitals in New York City ranged from a low of $50 to a high of $87. The range among 42 New York City community hospitals was $34 to $61. Among a group of 12 hospitals carefully chosen for high-quality care, costs per patient-day ranged from $46 to $96, *after* wage scales had been adjusted to a common basis.[8] The American Hospital Association compiled operational data on 431 hospitals of different sizes throughout

7. I am ignoring a third aspect of cost reduction, namely, better regional planning of hospital facilities, especially with respect to economies of scale in the provision of specialized high-cost services (for example, renal dialysis).

8. All of these data are cited in *Report of the National Advisory Commission on Health Manpower*, Vol. I, p. 55.

the nation and found substantial economies of scale: small hospitals averaged 3.7 laboratory procedures per man-hour, large hospitals averaged 8.9; small hospitals annually averaged 1,829 patient-days per administration employee, large hospitals 4,128; small hospitals produced 3.9 meals per man-hour, large hospitals 5.5.[9] While some of this huge variance in costs among hospitals is associated with differences in the quality of care, much of it is undoubtedly traceable to differences in efficiency.

Recognizing both the problems and the opportunities afforded by the existence of Medicare and Medicaid, the administration sought and the Congress in 1967 granted the government authority to undertake experimental incentive reimbursement schemes. The difficulties in such an undertaking are too involved even to be summarized. But systematic analysis can and must play a major role in designing incentive reimbursement formulas, through analysis, classification, and measurement of output.

We seek a means to reduce hospital costs per unit of output. We do not seek a reduction in per diem costs achieved by producing poorer quality care. A number of schemes have been suggested for incentive reimbursement. For example, payment might be based on a regional average cost. Hospitals with higher costs than the regional average would have to absorb part of the excess; hospitals with lower costs would be allowed to share part of the savings. Incentives would thereby be introduced for each hospital to reduce costs. Over the long run, hospitals of more than average efficiency would be able to accumulate internal funds for expansion and to demonstrate to lenders that their cash flow could amortize borrowings, while inefficient hospitals would not. An alternative scheme is to

9. Cited in Herman M. Somers and Anne R. Somers, *Medicare and the Hospitals* (Brookings Institution, 1967), p. 237.

113

reimburse each hospital initially on the basis of its own costs, but to reward it for reducing costs toward the regional average and penalizing it in contrary cases.

Incentive schemes, however, will ultimately prove viable only to the extent that we can distinguish changes in cost for a constant quality of output from changes in cost associated with changes in quality. The National Advisory Commission on Health Manpower has suggested the establishment of peer review panels—groups of physicians, hospital administrators, and other professional personnel who would review the quality of care and evaluate the quality and utilization of services.[10] While this approach appears to have much merit, and may become an indispensable part of any incentive reimbursement scheme, it needs to incorporate criteria for evaluation. The range of services provided by a hospital is too complex and diverse to be evaluated as a lump, particularly when the evaluation is for the purpose of establishing payment for those services. Systematic analysis of hospital care directed toward establishing output-oriented functions or categories is a prerequisite for the establishment of meaningful evaluation criteria for peer review panels, or for any other quality evaluation mechanism. I am convinced that imaginative reimbursement mechanisms must be developed as a means for channeling private incentives in the direction of more efficient hospital care. But I am also convinced that systematic analysis of hospital functions will play a large role in the success of those mechanisms.

Incentives are important not only for the efficient, internal operation of hospitals, but also for the efficient utilization of expensive hospital services by doctors and patients. For decades, the typical private health insurance plan limited coverage to

10. *Report of the National Advisory Commission on Health Manpower*, Vol. I, pp. 46–48.

expenses incurred in the hospital. The incentive for excessive use of hospital services is obvious, strengthened by the fact that for the average physician, treatment of patients in the hospital is much more convenient than at home. An analysis of hospitalization experience, comparing federal employees covered by hospitalization insurance with those covered by prepaid comprehensive care plans (which have no built-in incentives for excessive hospitalization) dramatically illustrates the effects of incentives. Between 1961 and 1965, hospital utilization rates of federal employees covered by hospital insurance plans rose by 35 to 45 percent. Rates for employees covered by prepaid comprehensive plans were much lower to begin with and did not rise at all during this period.[11]

Under Medicare and Medicaid, which cover both hospital and physicians' costs, some of the perverse incentives for excess hospitalization are removed. With a few exceptions, the patient has no financial incentive for excessive hospitalization, as compared to treatment at home, in outpatient clinics, or in the doctor's office. But, since payment to physicians is separate from payments to hospitals, the incentive for the physician to commit patients to the hospital remains. Neither patient nor doctor directly bears the excess costs. Where medical service is organized on a comprehensive group care basis, this incentive is substantially decreased since the excessive costs of hospital care use up much of the premium paid the group for overall medical care. Rapid expansion of group medical practice is inhibited, however, by both the strong desire of many patients for choosing an individual doctor and the medical profession's strong preference for the "fee-for-service" concept of payment. Recognizing these facts, it seems to me that there is room to

11. *Ibid.*, p. 67, Figure 7.

experiment with various reimbursement schemes designed to neutralize incentives for excessive hospital utilization, while still preserving fee-for-service concepts. But these experiments will have to be based on careful analysis of the structure of medical care and delivery systems. What is important is recognizing the need to devise systems that channel incentives toward efficient utilization.

I have attempted to cover a complex subject in a very few words. And to the professionals who have labored in this field for many years, I apologize for the inevitable oversimplification. But payment for medical care offers one of the most striking examples of the need for analysis in the design of systems that channel and direct private incentives toward the achievement of public goals.

Manpower Training

During the last three years, federal manpower training programs have gradually been reoriented toward the training and placement of the hard-core disadvantaged in the inner city. At the same time, the difficulties of running individual training projects in thousands of communities throughout the country have become more apparent. Training projects have tended to be small in size. They have often involved the signing of hundreds of individual contracts, each for a small number of trainees, each with excessively high costs, and many with limited access to large employers who could be the prime users of trained personnel. Conflicting organizations and groups have sprung up, each receiving some form of federal aid and attempting to train and place a relatively small number of people.

Toward the end of 1967, the administration joined with a nation-wide group of businessmen in launching a new approach to this problem. The program, now in its initial stages, involves signing relatively large contracts with business firms, turning over to those firms the entire content of a training program—recruitment, orientation, counseling, training, and job experience. Negotiated contracts cover not only the costs of these activities but to some extent the loss in productivity associated with the employment of unskilled trainees. Among its other objectives, this program seeks to substitute wholesale operations for retail operations.[12] Federal administrators cannot effectively oversee the design and operation of all the individually designed programs in each community. But they can design the contractual techniques and requirements that will use private incentives to achieve the same purposes.

As experience is gained in this program, there will emerge a need for the development of incentive contracting techniques. In turn, this will require a careful definition of the specific outputs desired by the program, and the design of contract rewards and penalties which relate performance to the initial capabilities of the trainees. Current contracts do have some simple incentives built in. Total contract payments per trainee are divided into twelve equal installments, and paid to the contractor monthly for as long as the trainee is employed. Since there are a number of fixed costs involved, the marginal cost of an additional month's employment is less than one-twelfth of total costs. Hence, there is an incentive to keep the trainee for a significant period of time. But more sophisticated definitions of desired output are needed in terms of employment, income, and the characteristics of trainees. Incentive contracting requires careful thinking through and specification of desired performance.

12. This distinction is used by Robert A. Levine, "Rethinking Our Social Strategies," *The Public Interest*, No. 10 (Winter 1968), pp. 86–96. Levine stresses the desirability of developing incentive systems to make possible a much greater decentralization of decision making in federal social programs.

Urban Development

Both the federal government and city governments have struggled for years with the problem of planning urban development. Almost every form of federal assistance to municipalities is conditioned on some kind of planning requirement—comprehensive plans, functional plans, planning processes, social renewal plans, workable programs, and so on. But, all too often, the plans are more breached than observed. In large part this occurs because the system of rewards and penalties connected with urban investment runs precisely counter to the goals and objectives of the plan.

The combined impact of capital gains taxation and economic rent on patterns of urban development is one of the best examples of the conflict between private incentives and public objectives. The typical metropolitan urban plan projects urban growth along radial lines that emanate outward from the central city, with high density occupancy along the spokes and lighter density in between. The advantages of this pattern for the economic development of urban mass transit systems are obvious. In addition, zoning regulations are often based on this planned density mix. But as high density development occurs along the spokes, the potential return from high density development of land between the spokes begins to rise. Owners of land in that area are blocked from larger and larger capital gains by zoning regulations. Moreover, whereas profit returned on physical improvements is essentially insensitive to density characteristics and is taxed at normal rates, the profit available from foresighted purchase of land is positively related to the density of development and is further enhanced by advantageous capital gains taxation. Zoning regulations cannot withstand the pressure of economic incentives that are accentuated by the tax system.

The same kind of perverse incentives contributes to the creation of urban blight. Why invest funds to improve decaying, downtown slum property? The return on such an investment is subject to the normal tax rate. But by investing in property simply to hold for future price increases, returns can be taken in the form of capital gains. Moreover, slum buildings can often be depreciated several times over in the process, as each sale creates a new taxable basis. Pouring tax money into urban renewal, to rectify what federal, state, and local tax laws have created, is scarcely a profitable enterprise. Indeed, nothing would be more effective in arresting urban decay and suburban sprawl than taking the profit out of promoting them.

None of this is new. My objective, however, is to suggest that systematic analysis dealing with urban development concentrate less on designing ideal plans and more on developing workable measures of taxation to direct private incentives closer to socially desirable objectives.

Grant Programs

In fiscal 1969, federal grants-in-aid to state and local governments are scheduled to exceed $20 billion, exactly double what they were five years earlier. These grants are directed toward a wide variety of specific purposes. In January 1966—the latest date for which an actual count has been made—there were 162 major grant programs. In many cases, individual programs have within them several different types of grant authorizations —for training, for operations, for research, and so forth. In early 1966, the number of these grant authorizations was 399; since then the number has mounted.[13] Presumably, these grant

13. "Federal Aid to State and Local Governments," *Special Analyses, Budget of the United States, Fiscal Year 1969* (1968), p. 164.

programs were not designed simply to provide generalized financial assistance to state and local governments. Each is the result of a relatively complex piece of legislation, aimed at a particular set of objectives.

In some cases, federal programs have been directed toward purposes for which state and local governments have historically spent little funds. In these situations federal funds for a particular purpose have undoubtedly been effective in increasing total resources devoted to that purpose. The Office of Economic Opportunity's program to provide legal services for the poor is such an example. At the other extreme, however, federal funds in many grant programs represent only a small fraction of state, local, or private outlays already devoted to the objective which the federal grant program seeks to foster. Title I grants for elementary and secondary education and subsidized loans for the construction of college housing facilities are such examples. In too few cases is there any positive evidence of the extent to which the individual programs have increased the *total* resources flowing to the programmed objective. We do not know the extent to which federal funds simply substitute for funds that the state and local governments would otherwise have spent for a particular purpose.

The federal college housing loan program, for example, provides long-term federal loans at 3 percent to public and private institutions for construction of housing facilities. For every $25 million provided by federal loans, living quarters for 5,000 students can be constructed. Given current interest rates on tax-exempt bonds, the lower interest rate made available by the federal government reduces room rent by $6 to $7 per month for students at publicly supported institutions of higher education. Recent estimates of the income distribution of students attending public universities show that approximately 45 percent come from families with incomes above $10,000 per year. Estimates of income for those students who board away from home are not available. But the proportion from families with income above $10,000 is probably higher at such schools. Under these circumstances it is quite likely that a large proportion of the subsidy involved in the college housing program simply substitutes for funds that these families, not in the lower-income group, would have spent. Yet the net cash expenditures for this program currently amount to over $300 million per year.[14] The expenditure of these funds may be desirable. But to the extent that the program's objective is to increase the flow of funds into higher education, and not merely to subsidize college housing for the sons and daughters of middle- and upper-income groups, the question of whether federal program funds are substitutable or additive to state, local, and private funds is highly relevant.[15]

In federal grant-in-aid programs, systematic analysis needs to give much more attention to the problem of designing program structures to maximize the additivity of federal funds. The grant-in-aid programs should presumably contain incentive provisions to insure that its objectives are attained, at least in the minimum sense of channeling additional resources toward the purposes for which the program was enacted. If the sole purpose of the grant-in-aid program is to ease the financial burden on state and local governments, then revenue sharing or

14. The long-term cost to the federal government is, of course, less than the initial capital outlay, since the loans are repayable. But the immediate effect of the program is to draw over $300 million from a tightly constrained budget.

15. One might object that without the federal college housing program many colleges would be unable to float the necessary bonds, in the private market, even if charges for board were set to fully amortize those bonds. But if the program's objective was simply to insure that adequate financing was available, it could be handled with little charge to the federal budget by providing federal guarantees of private bond flotations at market rates of interest.

121

similar means are available as a more effective and less expensive way of doing so.

Other Applications

I have illustrated only a few areas where the design of incentive systems promises to yield large payoffs. There are countless others. In the field of water pollution, for example, the use of effluent charges as a levy against pollutors, graduated on the basis of the pollutants they discharge into waterways, offers an effective means of abating pollution. One of the major advantages of effluent charges is that they provide automatic incentives for industries to redesign their internal production processes to reduce pollution. This is often much less expensive than building waste treatment plants to clean up pollution once it has occurred. In a study of the Delaware River estuary, it was found that it would be about 40 percent cheaper to reach a given standard of water quality by inducing selective waste reduction through the use of effluent charges than by requiring equal-proportional treatment of all wastes.[16] The typical steel plant uses 40,000 to 50,000 gallons of water per ton of steel, and contributes accordingly to pollution. But the Kaiser steel plant at Fontana, California, where water prices tend to be higher than in many other parts of the nation, uses only 1,500 gallons of water per ton of steel.[17] The volume of pollutants discharged by the paper industry can vary by a factor of 20 to 1, depending on the production process, the product mix, and the raw materials used. As in other cases, the design of effluent

16. Federal Coordinating Committee on the Economic Impact of Pollution Abatement, "Cost Sharing with Industry?" Summary Report, Revised (processed; Executive Office Building, 1967), p. 20.

17. Jack Hirshleifer, James C. DeHaven, and Jerome W Milliman, *Water Supply: Economics, Technology and Policy* (University of Chicago Press, 1960), p. 27.

charge systems requires a careful analysis of program objectives and outputs in terms of water quality and patterns of industrial location. The most efficient mix of effluent charges, waste treatment facilities, and other control measures depends in part upon the particular set of objectives chosen.

Elementary and secondary education, particularly compensatory education in the inner city, desperately needs development of incentive systems. At the present time, the educational system in the inner city is virtually a complete monopoly with a captive market. Schools tend to be judged on inputs—the quality and income level of students, the pupil-teacher ratio, the number of library books per student, and so forth. Outputs are hard to define and too often seem to be treated as irrelevant. Incentive systems of all kinds need to be developed and tried in experimental form. The City of Philadelphia, for example, recently considered the use of an incentive scheme that bases the pay of school principals on certain highly desired outputs— reduction in the dropout rate, improvement in percentile ranking on achievement tests, and the like. This aroused vociferous opposition and has not been carried out. A number of more fundamental proposals have been advanced to confront the present monopoly with competition. These include the radical proposals of Milton Friedman to convert the public school system to a private system, paying tuition grants to parents,[18] and the more moderate suggestion of James Coleman to provide tuition grants to be used for "purchasing" special courses from private contractors.[19] Expanding on the variety of current proposals for granting substantial autonomy to school

18. Milton Friedman, "The Role of Government in Education," in Robert Solo (ed.), *Economics and the Public Interest* (Rutgers University Press, 1955).

19. James S. Coleman, "Towards Open Schools," *The Public Interest*, No. 9 (Fall 1967), pp. 20–27.

districts in city neighborhoods, Henry Levin has suggested a modified approach: to allow each district to seek bids from contractors for designing and managing parts of neighborhood school systems.[20] My point, however, is not to show the merits or faults of any particular proposal. What is important is to open up a line of investigation and experimentation with the use of incentives to improve performance, and the corollary observation that these approaches all require an explicit analysis of the objectives and the outputs of programs producing public goods.

While I have stressed the desirability of developing incentive systems across a wide range of governmental activities, I do not want to leave the impression that this can easily be accomplished. Incentive schemes must be carefully analyzed to insure that unintended side effects are not produced. In designing an incentive contract for manpower training programs, for example, we must be careful that incentives paid for employment and income results do not lead contractors to skim the cream of the unemployed labor pool. A flood control insurance program in which the premium structure is seriously out of line with the risk structure will lead to overdevelopment or underdevelopment of flood plains, depending on which way the premium structure is awry. Even with a premium structure matched to risk, failure to charge beneficiaries for the cost of public works for flood control will set up strong political pressures for uneconomic investments, since those investments would immediately and directly reduce premiums paid by beneficiaries. Incentive schemes must also distinguish events which are under the control of those receiving incentive payments from those which are not.

20. Henry M. Levin, "The Failure of the Public Schools and the Free Market Remedy," *The Urban Review*, Vol. 2, No. 7 (June 1968), pp. 32–37 (Brookings Reprint 148).

An attempt to construct incentive payment schemes for school principals based on certain output measures, such as reducing dropout rates, must be able to distinguish changes in dropout rates caused by shifts in the socioeconomic composition of the neighborhood from changes induced by the school system. Effluent charges, to be economically meaningful, must take into account seasonal and other variations in stream flow, since the damages from a given quantity of effluents vary substantially with stream flow. Moreover, it is impossible to devise meaningful incentive systems if those subject to the system are not free to change the input mix of their operation. There is little point to an incentive manpower contract if other portions of the contract specify the precise form and content of training. Incentives for school administrators are meaningless if rigid teacher certification requirements, course curricula, and other input specifications are strictly controlled by a higher authority. For all of these reasons, the development of incentive systems demands careful thought and reliance on carefully evaluated experiments.

In summary, I am convinced that the increasing complexity of governmental social programs, the growing political demands for "participatory democracy," and considerations of sheer efficiency all call for a sharp increase in decentralized incentive programs. At the same time, however, the design of such programs will tax our limited analytical capability. Although the objective of incentive systems is to reduce the role of centralized planning in the detailed management of programs, the design of such systems requires painstaking ex ante analysis and experiment to insure, so far as possible, that the rewards and penalties do not produce perverse results.

125

7 Political and Administrative Improvements

The chief burden of these lectures has been to demonstrate how systematic analysis can adapt itself to the realities of the political process. I think it only fitting that they should be concluded by turning the coin around. Analysis of the major domestic problems facing the nation points to certain deficiencies in our current political and administrative decision processes. There are no easy means of correcting these deficiencies, but analysis can, I believe, suggest the general direction that improvements could take. Let me describe briefly several of these problem areas, which are closely related to each other.

The Relationship of Political Boundaries to External Benefits and Costs

The distinguishing characteristic of what I have called a quasi-public good is that the production or consumption of the good entails significant external benefits or costs. That is, the benefits to society are greater than the benefits enjoyed by the individual consumer, or the costs to society are greater than the costs incurred by individual producers. In such a situation, market price and cost signals cannot be accurate and, consequently, purely private production and consumption decisions will result in too little or too much of the good. The quantity of a good, however, is not always the central issue. Education is an example where the problem is the quality of the good. Public programs are inaugurated either to produce a good directly or to influence the quantity or quality produced privately.

The basic raison d'être for any public goods program relates to external costs and benefits; the public bodies making program decisions should take into account these costs and benefits.[1] But if the boundaries of the political body are not roughly

1. I do not mean this to be a counsel of perfection. It is neither possible nor

congruent with the boundaries over which the external benefits
or costs prevail, decisions will be biased and inefficient. If the
affected area is too small, important benefits or costs will be
ignored. If the area is too large, excessive centralization and the
associated inefficiencies will result.

The problem is clearly illustrated in the central cities of larger
metropolitan areas. The discrepancy between the universe of
those who receive benefits from central city services and the
sources of central city revenue has been analyzed, discussed,
publicized, and debated for decades. But there is another aspect
to the problem: relevant political boundaries differ for different
public goods. Some public goods have a *wider* boundary of external benefits and costs than others, but more important, they
often have *overlapping* boundaries. This is not a problem of con-
centric circles, but of intersecting circles.

Analysis of water pollution abatement suggests particular
geographic boundaries that are relevant to decisions of water
pollution control. And, in general, those boundaries are dictated
by water flows, so that watersheds and river basins become
suitable political decision entities. External benefits and costs
of air pollution dictate airsheds as relevant decision units. But
airsheds and watersheds do not coincide. The planning and
financing of urban transportation systems involve external
benefits and costs roughly related to commuter distances—and
this has little relationship to either watersheds or airsheds.
Policies to assist the economic development of depressed areas
should be formulated on the basis of functional economic areas,
and often this will involve commuter areas distributed around
economic growth centers. But this is not always the case. On

---

desirable to try to consider all of the consequences of a decision. But the *major*
externalities that give rise to public programs must be considered.

the other hand, planning and executing many social services can often be most effectively undertaken by public bodies whose boundaries are smaller than the municipality.[2]

If we accept the conclusion that technical and economic considerations require different, and overlapping, jurisdictional boundaries for different problems, we are immediately faced with some major political dilemmas. Most current political boundaries have little relationship to the technical nature of the problems to be considered. These facts seem to point to the establishment of special political authorities, whose jurisdictions are determined by the nature of the public good, and whose powers are limited to decisions about that particular good. But, at least in its raw form, this is an illusory escape from the problem. First, special authorities often acquire semiautonomous, self-perpetuating status, and become political eunuchs, with only a tenuous connection to the electorate. Second, in many cases, external benefits or costs of public goods are unevenly distributed over the relevant geographic area. In the case of water pollution, upstream pollutors cause damages to downstream water users. A river basin system of effluent charges, graduated to damages caused by pollution, would, generally, fall much more heavily on upstream water users than downstream users, while a basin-wide plan for waste treatment

2. I am not suggesting that all of the external benefits and costs of a particular program are confined to a single set of boundaries. The externalities relevant to the choice of decision boundaries are the ones that most directly affect or are affected by the technical nature of program design. In the case of water pollution control, for example, programs should be designed in a river basin or watershed framework. Some external benefits from abatement may, nevertheless, accrue to the nation as a whole, justifying transfer payments to accelerate abatement schemes. In the case of elementary and secondary schools, it may turn out that many program decisions can be made by neighborhood school districts. Yet national external benefits would still justify transfer payments for increasing the scale and intensity of compensatory education.

facilities would tend to benefit downstream users more than upstream users. Thus, it is unlikely that upstream communities will be eager to join single-purpose special authorities, in which they gain little but pay much. Similarly a program designed to promote economic development by concentrating infrastructure investment in urban growth centers is not likely to be embraced by officials and voters in outlying rural counties. Even though this strategy for the development of depressed areas may ultimately prove beneficial to those counties, passing up immediate state and federal development loans and grants requires greater foresight than most of us possess. In short, decision-making bodies whose jurisdictions are determined by the geography of benefits and costs and whose authority is limited to decisions about a particular public good may often be rendered impotent by the fact that the component communities are sharply split between clear gainers and clear losers.

There is no easy answer to these kinds of problems. But certain changes can be made in government organization and the political process that might ease the problem. Before discussing them, I will describe two other organizational problems that call for the same kinds of changes.

There are a number of substantive characteristics of the federal government's rapidly growing domestic social programs that raise massive problems for the decision-making process.

First, attacking the problems involved in the inner city requires not just a single policy instrument, but many; education, jobs, housing, health, transportation, law enforcement are all involved. The success of compensatory education, for example, is not unrelated to the availability of jobs for the parents of school children or the prospect of jobs for high school graduates. The effective delivery of medical services in the inner city is related in part to the training and use of inner city residents as

130

subprofessional medical personnel. In the model cities programs a single application for assistance will involve drawing upon a wide range of federal resources and grants, administered by a number of different federal agencies. Budgetary resources must be reserved for each of these components. For any individual department, however, these grants to model city neighborhoods are only a part of a larger functional program. Similarly, water pollution abatement in a river basin brings in the Corps of Engineers, the Interior Department, the Department of Agriculture, and the Public Health Service. Assistance to accelerate the development of economically depressed areas involves investment planning by many federal agencies. The interdependence of these programs requires the concerted action of many government departments and agencies that are organizationally independent of each other.

Second, in its newer social programs the federal government is directly involved in program decisions at the local level in thousands of individual communities throughout the nation. And even if decision making is highly decentralized, with local programs being designed at the local level, decisions on the scope and level of federal participation and approval of federal grants require that decisions be made in the field. Unlike more traditional programs—defense, agricultural price support, veterans' benefits, straight formula grants-in-aid, and the like—policy coordination at the Washington level, difficult as that is, is no longer enough.

Third, all of the newer federal social programs are joint ventures with state, county, and city governments—in some cases with all of them at the same time. In any program involving both education and health, for example, a Head Start program including medical examinations for the children paid for by Medicaid, it is necessary to involve at least two federal departments, the local school board, the state-controlled public health service, the city welfare department, and the local community action agency.

Dealing with this incredible array of political jurisdictions and different but coequal agencies within the same jurisdiction poses tremendous problems for decision making. Much of the difficulty is inherent in a system where a multiplicity of governments is encouraged. But much of it also comes from the functional organization of the federal government. Combining different functional components into a single program package is difficult enough on a national basis, but when it must be done in thousands of communities among coequal departments of a number of political jurisdictions, the difficulties increase by orders of magnitude.

The problem for the federal government is that it has no regional structure as a government. It is functionally organized with individual lines of authority running parallel to each other directly from Washington to the field. Even within individual cabinet departments, there is no meaningful regional authority for the department as a whole. Individual bureaus have independent field establishments, not responsible to any overall departmental official in a region or a city. Thus, the organization of the federal government has not caught up with the substantive nature of the problem it faces. It is attempting to deal with regional social problems through comprehensive programs that combine a host of different elements. On the organizational side, it has no overall regional structure. It has no good regional mechanism to plan, allocate budget resources, and handle day-to-day operating conflicts among the different functional units whose programs must be combined in a single package. Moreover, local officials who seek control of their own departmental bureaucracy have no one to deal with. The state and local functional bureaucracies deal directly with their federal counter-parts in negotiating federal aid; there is no federal government at the regional level, only a series of independent federal agencies.

The federal government needs to develop a regional struc-ture—a regional presence as a government. Not only must indi-vidual departments strengthen the power of their regional officials but, more important, the Executive Office of the Presi-dent needs a regional presence. A mediating presence need not and should not be a regional "czar" over all federal agencies, but rather someone to coordinate related federal programs at the local level; someone who can assist mayors and governors in carrying out, with the federal government, joint enterprises, in which education, training, slum rehabilitation, and public facilities each forms part of a comprehensive program. There are many forms this regional presence could take. There are also many problems in determining the appropriate powers to be granted the regional representatives of the executive office and their departmental colleagues. Moreover, there are formidable political obstacles toward moving in this direction. Such a move would tend to strengthen the power of mayors and governors with respect to local programs of the federal government and, accordingly, would weaken the informal power of Congress. Individual congressional subcommittees exert substantial power through their influence on the Washington headquarters of functional bureaus. To the extent that these bureaus delegate more power to the field, and that the actions of those bureau field officials become subject to review by departmental and executive office regional officials, the link between congressional subcommittees and particular executive decisions would be weakened.

I cannot predict or prescribe the particular nature of the

necessary regionalization. It must be approached gradually and experimentally. I do believe that a regional structure for the federal government is a major necessity. It must have sufficient power to deal with problems that arise among coequal federal agencies. It must permit the *geographic decentralization* of decisions from Washington to the field that local conditions demand and political good sense dictates. But it must also permit a *functional centralization* of decisions that the interrelated nature of federal programs requires.

There is a second important kind of political and organizational problem which a move toward regionalism might help alleviate. At the present time one of the most difficult problems in budgetary allocation is what I shall call, for want of a better term, "functional logrolling." By that I mean that it is difficult to enact programs, particularly those of a public investment character, that are targeted to a specific geographically limited problem. Federal investment programs, designed to meet specific problems of the inner city, are broadened by congressional amendments to include rural areas. Conversely, programs targeted to specific rural needs are often broadened to include metropolitan areas. There is no means by which bargains can be made to provide one kind of functional assistance for one area and another kind of assistance for other areas. Each functional program tends to be broadened to include all areas, whether they need it or not. The present legislative process, and the packaging of administration proposals, encourages logrolling of projects strictly within functional lines.

In 1964, for example, the administration proposed a limited sewer and water grant-in-aid program based on the premise that the development of rapidly growing suburban communities was being too heavily dictated by private land speculators and developers. But, it was hypothesized, if such communities could build sewer and water lines before development took place, they could more easily control the pattern of growth in accordance with their own development plans. A bill for a grant program to furnish them with the funds for this plan was written. But the Congress refused to pass a bill that provided grants to such a restricted set of beneficiaries. It broadened eligibility substantially, so that a large proportion of all sewer and water investment in the United States became eligible.

Authorization for public works projects suffers from this same problem. There is no mechanism by which congressmen and communities can forego pressing for a marginal public works project in return for a vocational education project, or a hospital, or some other federally aided investment which may have a much higher payoff to the community. Concentration of economic assistance to potential urban growth centers in economically depressed areas is making slow progress because local interests cannot trade off across functional lines. Congress views decisions function by function. Generally, because public investment tradeoffs are made in a functional perspective rather than in a regional one, it is difficult to design acceptable functional programs which are geographically selective in character.

It is my view that the development of a more meaningful regional structure for the federal government may ultimately lead to a partial solution of this problem. Within a regional framework, it may become possible for the political process to make better decisions involving geographical selectivity. I pointed out earlier the problem of special authorities covering an area whose boundaries were different than those of general purpose governments. Such authorities often pit clear gainers against clear losers because they deal with single functional decisions. But with the development of a regional federal structure, it may be possible to put together multifunctional pack-

135

ages. Communities or areas which are "losers" in one set of functional investment decisions may be "gainers" in another one. Multifunctional programs may mitigate political tradeoff problems. Political pressures on congressmen and the administration to maximize the federal aid flowing to a given area will always remain with us. But within that constraint, regionalism may make it possible to widen the area of choice and encourage local areas to select more efficient projects.

An increase in regionalism, however, involves countless questions of policy, of execution, of organization, and of procedural steps. Regionalization must be gradual, and it will be because it is politically so difficult. It should be a limited move: the regional approach should not obliterate the functional since both have roles to play.[3] But despite all the unanswered questions—indeed because of them—I believe that further thought and consideration could profitably be devoted toward exploring the detailed steps and procedures that regionalization might take.

Conclusion

In the last two chapters there have been many different threads. Yet I believe they form the outline of a pattern. The complexity of the social problems with which the nation is now grappling and their variety from community to community call for both a

3. Herbert Kaufman, in discussing the regionalization of the federal government, predicts that it will occur, that it will be a healthy development, that it will ultimately go too far in "politicizing" technical decisions, and that the cycle will eventually swing back toward restoring some of the powers of functional bureaus. But he also points out that in this cyclical development gains will probably be made and retained, in terms of a more effective governmental process. See Herbert Kaufman, "Administrative Decentralization and Political Power" (paper prepared for delivery at the 1968 annual meeting of the American Political Science Association; processed).

national commitment of resources and strong local participation in the use of those resources. Federal programs must be skillfully designed and federal budget resources carefully allocated if the government programs are to be effective. But skillful design and careful budgeting of national programs is not synonymous with central dictation of program detail. Rather, I believe, the program analyst should be called upon to help design incentive systems, processes and structures within which detailed decisions about program input mix can be made on a decentralized basis. I am also convinced that design and execution of federal social programs can be substantially improved by strengthening the regional structure of the federal government in relation to its functional components. And that regional structure should include, as a component, some form of regional executive office presence.

In these conclusions I have made proposals of a highly generalized nature. I do not have a detailed design to propose, nor an accurate map of the terrain ahead. I have made suggestions that may, upon closer investigation, prove to be illusory, if not downright dangerous. Yet, in reward for several years of poring over detailed budget figures and acting the role of professional skeptic, a recently retired budget director should be allowed a modest license to try a few of those venturesome leaps in the dark normally reserved for philosophers and politicians. I rest my defense on that justification.

Index